WILDFLOWERS
of MOUNT
RAINIER

Laird R. Blackwell

Lone Pine Publishing

The Publisher: Lone Pine Publishing

10145 – 81 Ave.   1901 Raymond Ave. SW, Suite C
Edmonton, AB T6E 1W9   Renton, WA 98055
Canada   USA

Website: www.lonepinepublishing.com

Canadian Cataloguing in Publication Data

Blackwell, Laird R. (Laird Richard), 1945-
   Wildflowers of Mount Rainier

Includes index.
   ISBN 1-55105-230-X

   1. Wild flowers--Washington (State)--Mount Rainier
Region--Identification. I. Title.
QK192.B52 2000   582.13'09797'782   C99-911314-3

Editorial Director: Nancy Foulds
Project Editor: Erin McCloskey
Editorial: Erin McCloskey, Randy Williams
Technical Review: Ron Warfield
Production Manager: Jody Reekie
Book Design: Heather Markham
Cover Design: Rob Weidemann
Layout & Production: Heather Markham, Monica Triska
Illustration: Ian Sheldon
Photography: Laird R. Blackwell
Cartography: Rob Weidemann, Elliot Engley
Scanning, Separations & Film: Elite Lithographers Co. Ltd.

Cover photos by Laird R. Blackwell

Lone Pine Publishing acknowledges the financial support of the Government of Canada
through the Book Publishing Industry Development Program (BPIDP) for their publishing activities.

PC: P3

Contents

Dedication

To Melinda, my wife and soul-mate, who shares with me so much of what I love, who supports me in so much more, and who gently tolerates the rest. Sometimes these loves, like writing books, take me away for a short while, but I always come back even more in love with her.

Acknowledgements

To all my students through the years who have helped me see with fresh eyes. To the wonderful people at Lone Pine Publishing who have accompanied me now on three delicious wildflower journeys. To Ron Warfield, retired Assistant Chief Park Naturalist at Mt. Rainier National Park, for his careful and intelligent reading and critique of the manuscript. To the flowers for holding nothing back, and to the grand old mountain for sharing her majesty with such generosity of spirit.

Pictorial Index to Flowers

by color and petal number

White: 3/6

Western trillium
p. 35

Queen's cup
p. 36

Clasping twisted
stalk p. 37

Hooker's fairybell
p. 38

Heart-leaf
twayblade p. 39

Rattlesnake
plantain p. 40

Plumose false
Solomon's seal
p. 66

Slender bog
orchid p. 67

Avalanche lily
p. 117

Beargrass
p. 118

Green false
hellebore p. 141

White: 4

Canadian
dogwood p. 41

False lily-of-the-
valley p. 68

Mountain sorrel
p. 99

Smelowskia
p. 161

Pussy paws
p. 175

5

White: 5

Single-flowered
Indian pipe p. 42

Candystick
p. 43

Salal
p. 44

Woodnymph
p. 45

One-sided
wintergreen p. 46

Kinnikinnick
p. 47

Foamflower
p. 48

Creeping
raspberry p. 49

Wild strawberry
p. 50

Devil's club
p. 51

Fringecup
p. 69

Brewer's
mitrewort p. 70

Brook saxifrage
p. 71

Thimbleberry
p. 81

Goat's beard
p. 82

Western
mountain ash
p. 83

Scouler's
harebell p. 84

Small-flowered
alumroot p. 100

Rusty saxifrage
p. 101

Sickletop
lousewort p. 119

White
rhododendron
p. 120

Sitka valerian
p. 121

Small-flowered
penstemon
p. 135

Bistort
p. 142

Cow parsnip
p. 143

Tolmie's
saxifrage p. 162

Elmera
p. 163

Arctic sandwort
p. 164

Partridge foot
p. 165

Newberry's
knotweed p. 166

Coiled-beak
lousewort p. 167

White mountain
heather p. 168

White: no/many

Spreading phlox
p. 179

Canadian
dogwood p. 41

Vanilla leaf
p. 52

Pathfinder
p. 53

False bugbane
p. 72

Pearly
everlasting p. 85

Columbia lewisia
p. 102

Pasqueflower
p. 122

7

Mountain daisy
p. 123

Marsh marigold
p. 144

Sweet coltsfoot
p. 145

Alpine pussytoes
p. 169

Yellow/Orange: 3/6

Pussy paws
p. 175

Cascade Oregon-
grape p. 54

Tiger lily
p. 86

Glacier lily
p. 124

Yellow/Orange: 5

Pine-sap
p. 55

Fringed pine-sap
p. 56

Tall yellow violet
p. 73

Round-leaf violet
p. 73

Oregon
stonecrop p. 103

Spreading
stonecrop p. 103

Bracted
lousewort p. 125

Fan-leaf
cinquefoil p. 126

Yellow/Orange: no/many

Mountain
monkeyflower
p. 146

Yellow mountain
heather p. 170

Shrubby
cinquefoil p. 171

Yellow skunk
cabbage p. 74

Orange agoseris
p. 87

Broadleaf arnica
p. 127

Alpine golden
daisy p. 172

Short-beaked
agoseris p. 173

Pink/Red: 3/6

Pink/Red: 4

Northern
goldenrod p. 174

Western
coralroot p. 57

Fairy slipper
p. 58

Fireweed
p. 88

Pink/Red: 5

Western
corydalis p. 89

Smoothstem
willow-herb
p. 147

Pussy paws
p. 175

Pipsissewa
p. 59

Pink wintergreen
p.60

Twinflower
p. 62

Cooley's
hedgenettle p. 90

Harsh paintbrush
p. 91

Woodland
penstemon p. 92

Foxglove
p. 93

Crimson
columbine p. 94

Salmonberry
p. 95

Self-heal
p. 96

Cliff penstemon
p. 104

Pennyroyal
p. 105

Pink mountain
heather p. 128

Cascade
huckleberry
p. 129

Rosy spirea
p. 130

Magenta
paintbrush p. 131

Jeffrey's
shooting star
p. 148

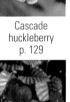
Lewis
monkeyflower
p. 149

Elephantheads
p. 150

Bog laurel
p. 151

Cliff paintbrush
p. 176

Pink/Red: no/many

Bird's-beak
lousewort p. 177

Moss campion
p. 178

Spreading phlox
p. 179

Pacific starflower
p. 63

Blue/Purple: 4

Columbia lewisia
p. 102

Mountain daisy
p. 123

Edible thistle
p. 132

Youth-on-age
p. 75

Blue/Purple: 5

Cusick's veronica
p. 152

Marsh violet
p. 79

Butterwort
p. 76

Tall bluebell
p. 77

Monkshood
p. 78

Self-heal
p. 96

Subalpine lupine
p. 133

Early blue violet
p. 134

Small-flowered
penstemon
p. 135

Common harebell
p. 136

Showy Jacob's
ladder p. 137

Mountain bog
gentian p. 153

Spreading phlox
p. 179

Davidson's
penstemon
p. 180

Alpine lupine
p. 181

Elegant Jacob's
ladder p. 182

Blue/Purple: no/many

Cascade aster
p. 138

Alpine aster
p. 183

Introduction

The highest peak in the Pacific Northwest and one of the grandest mountains on Earth, Mt. Rainier seems a world unto itself. At over 14,000' and soaring more than 8000' above the surrounding Cascades, it is a towering solitary beacon of snow and ice shining its light and allure for hundreds of miles in all directions.

Mt. Baker, Mt. Adams, Mt. St. Helens, Mt. Hood, Mt. Jefferson, Mt. Shasta, Lassen Peak, and other lone volcanic peaks are strung loosely along the strand of pearls that is the Cascade Range of Washington, Oregon, and northern California. Each peak has its own beauty and mystique, but Rainier is the pearl of pearls; it is the highest, the most massive, the most accessible, and is home to some of the world's most spectacular wildflower gardens.

From a distance Mt. Rainier, with all its gleaming snow and ice, is as forbidding in appearance as it is beautiful. The tree limit (the elevation above which no trees grow) here is at about 6500–7000', so more than 7000' of the mountain is above the 'land of trees' and is mostly covered in perpetual snow and ice. There are more glaciers on Mt. Rainier than on any other mountain in the United States excluding Alaska. Climbing high on the mountain among massive blocks of ice, deep crevasses, and falling rock is an awesome and humbling experience, but no more so than walking among the magnificent wildflower gardens at lower elevations.

Elevational Zones

When you enter Mt. Rainier National Park and get your first close-up view of the mountain, you see that it is much more than ice and snow. Its lower elevations (the **forest zone** from about 2000–5000') are cloaked in dense, lush, evergreen forests of pine, fir, Douglas-fir, spruce, hemlock, and cedar, which are home to a remarkable variety of flowering plants specially adapted to the forest environment. Blooming here generally starts in late April or May and reaches its peak in June or July. Coltsfoot and yellow skunk cabbage do the honors as the earliest bloomers at Rainer.

Above the forest zone is the **subalpine zone**, which extends from the 'forest line' (the upper limit of closed contiguous forest) at about 5000' to the tree limit (the elevation above which no trees grow) at about 7000'. This subalpine zone consists of individual trees, clumps of trees, and the rolling, open wildflower meadows for which Rainier is so famous. There are 2 major surges of blooming in these meadows: glacier lily, pasqueflower, marsh marigold, and a few others in late June and early July; and the majority of species in late July and August.

Although in Rainier you will often encounter permanent ice and snow just above the subalpine meadows, there are places where rocky ridges and gravelly flats extend far above the tree limit. This cold and windswept world is the **alpine zone**, where an amazing number of tenacious flowering plants can be found

CASCADE PEAKS

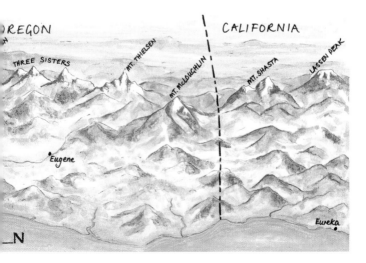

up to 8000'. Very few plants will be found higher than 8500'. Most of these alpine species bloom from late July through August or September.

A look at the diagram below of the elevational zones will show you that their elevations vary somewhat, depending on (among other things) what side of the mountain you are on. On most individual mountains in this region, the zones reach higher on the west and south sides, which are warmer than the east and north sides. On Mt. Rainier, however, the opposite is true with the zones reaching 500' or so higher on the north and east sides.

Mt. Rainier is so massive that it creates its own rain (and snow) shadow, so by the time the southwesterly storms reach

ELEVATIONAL ZONES

South & West Slopes

Alpine Zone

North & East Slopes

Tree Limit

6500'

7000'

Subalpine Zone

Forest Line

5300'

4800'

Forest Zone

the east and north sides of the mountain, they have already dumped much of their precipitation. There is still heavy snow on the east side, but nothing compared to that on the south and west sides. Whereas the average annual snowfall at Sunrise on the northeast side is about 300", at Paradise, 1000' lower but on the south side, it is over 600"! This difference in snowfall has a tremendous influence on the elevations of the zones. The lower limit of the subalpine zone (the forest line) is about 5300' on the Sunrise side and only about 4800' on the Paradise side; the lower limit of the alpine zone (the tree limit) is about 7000' on the Sunrise side and only about 6500' on the Paradise side.

This difference also shows up in the blooming of the flowers: in late July 1996, for example, snow was still covering most of the Paradise flower fields (the flowers were in bloom just above the parking lot at about 5400' but had not yet bloomed a few yards up the hill), while at Sunrise at 6400' the meadows were snowfree with flowers in full bloom.

The Mountain

Mt. Rainier, a towering volcanic cone of seemingly perpetual winter, turns out instead (on its lower half anyway) to be one of the most spectacular and diverse wildflower areas in the world. Whether you're tip-toeing through lush, primordial forests, meandering across emerald subalpine parks, scrambling up rocky ridges, or sitting quietly by one of the many streams or ponds, the wildflowers of Rainier call to you with their beauty. There is another call too—the enduring, haunting, compelling call of the mountain. Even when you can't see it, the mountain lingers in your thoughts as it looms over the land. The mountain is the source of all you see and feel, and the wonder in every petal and leaf.

How the Book is Organized

This book is divided into sections by elevational zones: the **forest zone**, the **subalpine zone**, and the **alpine zone** (see p. 15–16). The introduction to each section briefly describes the zone's characteristics, mentions some places you can drive or hike or backpack to experience that zone, and describes in more detail a featured trail that explores that zone.

The **forest** section is further divided into 4 special environments you will encounter frequently in the forest zone: 1) closed and open canopy forests, 2) wet areas, 3) clearings and open hillsides, and 4) rocky areas.

The **subalpine** section is further divided into 2 special environments you will frequently encounter in the subalpine zone: 1) open slopes and meadows, and 2) wet areas.

The **alpine** section is not further divided.

For more technical designations and discussions of Rainier plant communities and vegetative patterns see Henderson (1974), Edwards (1980), and Franklin (1988).

Each subsection in the forest and subalpine sections has a brief introduction that mentions places on the featured trail where you will find that environment.

The flower descriptions in each section or subsection are sequenced by color (from white to yellow to red to blue to brown). Within each color, flower descriptions are sequenced by petal number (3 or 6 to 4 to 5 to many or none). Each flower description includes common and scientific names, along with origins and meanings, family, flower and plant characteristics and special features, and blooming season. Typical location refers to the usual habitat in Rainier and a specific place, often along the featured trail, where you are likely to find the flower. Distribution is within North America.

At the beginning of the book you will find a pictorial index to the flowers, arranged by color and petal number. In the back of the book are indexes to common and scientific names.

How to Use the Book

Finding specific flowers is made easier with color keys, indexes, petal color and number categorizations as well as explanations of the elevational zones, typical locations, and trails where the flowers are found. Several approaches may be taken to help you locate and identify the flowers of Rainier:

1) Wherever you are in Mt. Rainier National Park, decide what elevational zone you're in and turn to that section of the book. Browse through the pages in that section or turn to the appropriate subsection (special environment) and thumb through those pages. The flowers within each environment subsection are arranged by petal number followed by color.

2) Read the introduction to one of the elevational zones and hike one of the trails mentioned as a good example of that zone. Use that section of the book to accompany your hike.

3) Hike the featured trail for a zone. The flower descriptions for that zone include specific places those flowers can be found on the featured trail.

4) To find a particular flower within the book, go to the typical location provided in the account.

5) Use the pictorial index at the beginning of the book, which organizes flowers by color and number of petals. When you find your flower, turn to the indicated page within the book.

6) If you know the flower's name, use the common name index or the scientific name index at the back of the book, then turn to the indicated page.

7) Thumb through all the pictures in the book until you find your flower.

8) Read the book in advance, so that when you find a flower, you will already have a good idea of what it is.

Enjoy and respect the land and the flowers. Picking flowers is not only thoughtless and selfish, but it is also illegal. Tramping through wildflower meadows can wreak havoc, so don't be a meadow stomper!

DO NOT TREAD. MOSEY, HOP, TRAMPLE. STEP. PLOD. TIPTOE. TROT. TRAIPSE. MEANDER. CREEP. PRANCE. AMBLE. JOG. TRUDGE. MARCH. STOMP. TODDLE. JUMP. STUMBLE. TROD. SPRINT. OR WALK ON PLANTS.

What Makes Rainier Flowers So Special

Few places in Rainier could be called dry. Although the lee (east and north) sides of the mountain get much less precipitation than the other sides, even they get plenty of snow and rain. The results on the landscape are obvious—rushing creeks and roaring rivers everywhere, dense forests and moss-covered rocks in lower elevations, lush green parks in subalpine elevations, and massive glaciers and snowfields higher up.

As for the flowers, they are incredibly profuse and intense in color.

Compared to the wildflower gardens of many other areas, Rainier's gardens are amazingly dense and extensive. The colors of its flowers seem to be just a notch brighter and more vibrant, a touch more intense, a hue deeper.

Lewis monkeyflower in the Sierra

Lewis monkeyflower in Rainier

21

Names

I t may seem that botanists are out to get you. Just when you learn the scientific names of plants, they are changed! Sometimes the change is the result of new knowledge from more sophisticated genetic analysis; sometimes it seems a bit more arbitrary. In this book I have used the most current scientific names (with recent former names in the names section and in the indexes).

Scientific names, though sometimes frustrating, are well worth learning because they can be interesting and revealing. The species names often describe a characteristic of the plant or give you a glimpse into the history of its discovery. The species names of the plants included in this book most frequently describe:

1) characteristics of the flower, e.g., *parviflora* (small), *grandiflorum* (large), *albiflorum* (white), *formosa* (beautiful), *aurantiaca* (red-orange), *dioicus* (separate male and female flowers)

2) characteristics of the leaves, e.g., *latifolia* (broad), *ovalifolium* (oval), *angustifolium* (narrow), *triphylla* (3-parted), *flabellifolia* (fan-shaped), *tenax* (tough)

3) characteristics of the plant, e.g., *divergens* (spreading), *peregrinus* (wandering), *procerus* (tall), *lanatum* (wooly), *horridum* (spiny)

4) characteristics of the fruit, e.g., *lasiococcus* (hairy), *deliciosus* (tasty)

5) environments or locations where the plant is found, e.g., *frigidus* (cold regions), *scopulina* (in the rocks), *hemorsa* (in the woods), *montanum* (in the mountains), *columbianum* (in western North America)

6) early explorers or plant collectors, e.g., *lewisia*, *scouleri*, *breweri*, *cusickii*, *menziesii*.

The genus names tend to be less helpful than the species names in distinguishing plant because, of course, these names may have originally been given to a species other than the one you're looking at. However, they sometimes point to a conspicuous characteristic of a plant that the entire genus shares, e.g., *Campanula* (little bell) or *Mimulus* (like a face). Often they honor a person. Sometimes the meaning of a genus name is obscure or unknown.

Once botanists come to agreement, these scientific names are consistent across geographic regions. This is certainly more than can be said of common names!

Often the same plant will have different common names in different parts of the country, e.g., *Gentiana calycosa* is usually called 'mountain bog gentian' in Rainier and in the rest of the Cascades but is called 'explorer's gentian' in the Sierra Nevada of California. Sometimes the same common name will be used in different parts of the country to refer to different plants, e.g., 'sky pilot' refers to *Polemonium elegans* in the Cascades but to *P. eximium* in the Sierra Nevada.

So, by all means enjoy the common names (and perhaps make up some new ones to help you remember and relate to the flower), but be aware of their limitations. You might want to take the trouble to learn the scientific names as well, for they certainly make communicating about flowers easier.

Mimulus

Forest Zone

(about 2000–5000')

The Pacific Northwest is renowned for its rich and diverse forests. Though Rainier does not have coastal rainforests, its lower elevations are thickly cloaked with luxuriant mixed-evergreen forests of various species of fir, pine, hemlock, spruce, and cedar.

At some of its lowest elevations (e.g., Carbon River) there are small patches of temperate rainforest boasting some of the world's largest and/or oldest members of several species. Though forests thin to make way for large meadows at elevations above about 5000', you will still find scattered clumps of trees and then some stunted or prostrate trees all the way up to the tree limit at about 7000'.

The deepest, darkest parts of the dense, closed canopy, low-elevation forests are home to a remarkable number of parasitic or saprophytic plants surviving in very limited sunlight by feeding off other plants. In more open areas of the forest—along creekbanks, rocky slopes, and large clearings—an even larger number of species of green-leaf flowering plants find congenial homes.

This forest section is divided into 4 special environments, each with its own specially adapted plants:

CLOSED & OPEN CANOPY

WET AREAS

CLEARINGS

ROCKY AREAS

Determine what kind of environment you're in and turn to the appropriate subsection of this book to find your flower.

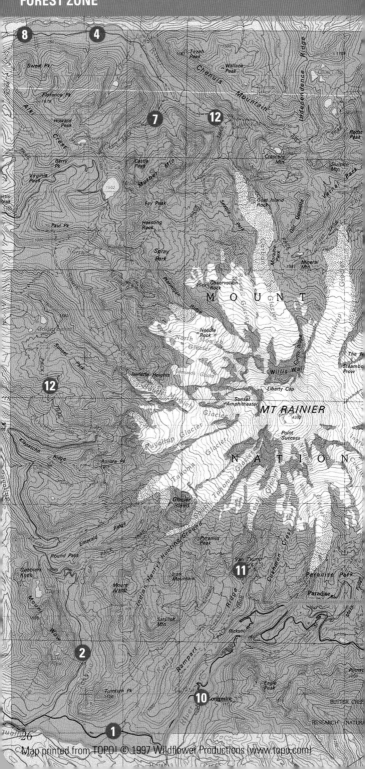

Map printed from TOPO! © 1997 Wildflower Productions (www.topo.com)

Most of the park's roads go through forests, but to really experience that mysterious, almost primordial feeling of the deep forest, you might want to drive one of the following park roads: ❶ from the Nisqually Entrance Station (in the southwest corner of the park at about 2000' elevation) to Longmire (at about 2700'), ❷ along the first few miles of the Westside Road branching off the Nisqually-Longmire Road, ❸ from Ohanapecosh (in the southeast corner at about 1900') to the Grove of the Patriarchs (at about 2200'), or ❹ from the Carbon River Entrance Station (in the northwest corner at about 1900') to Ipsut Creek (at about 2500').

Of course, to see the forest wildflowers up close, you will need to get out of your car and explore on foot. Many of the park's trails at least start (if not stay) in the deep, low-elevation forest. Some of the best such forest trails that are easily accessible include ❺ The Grove of the Patriarchs (1.5 miles of wandering through dense virgin forest of ancient Douglas-fir, western red cedar, and western hemlock), ❻ the East Side Trail (9 miles 1-way from Deer Creek to Ohanapecosh), ❼ Ipsut Creek (6 miles round-trip to the world's largest Alaska Yellow-Cedar), ❽ Carbon River (several short walks through temperate rain-forest), ❾ Nickel Creek (a 1-mile stroll from Box Canyon), ❿ any of the short trails in the Longmire and Cougar Rock areas, and ⓫ the Comet Falls Trail (see featured trail, p. 28). ⓬ Much of the 100-mile Wonderland Trail that circles the mountain is in the forest zone.

Featured Trail

COMET FALLS

(3.8 MILES ROUND-TRIP, ABOUT 1200' CLIMB)

Of all the wonderful trails that take you to the forest wildflowers, my favorite is the trail to Comet Falls (apparently it is many people's favorite, because the parking lot at the trailhead can be very crowded). Although this trail is not as low in elevation as many of the forest zone trails— it starts at 3600'—it spends most of its 1.9 miles to Comet Falls (at about 4800') meandering through a thick forest. But what makes this such a special trail for forest wildflowers is the variety of environments that you will encounter along it. You will come across deep woods, large clearings, bogs, seeps, and creekbanks, rock outcrops, and talus slopes. You will find almost all the flowers described in the forest section of this book right here along this trail.

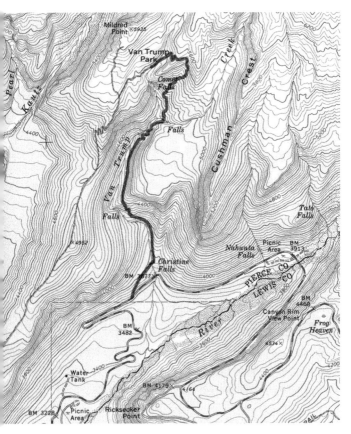

This trail parallels canyon-carving Van Trump Creek and will take you to 2 beautiful waterfalls and then continues a mile beyond Comet Falls up into the subalpine meadows of Van Trump Park.

Comet Falls

Vanilla leaf leaves

Special environments and flowers along featured trail: The trail to Comet Falls immediately enters dense forest; after a short climb from the parking lot, it levels off for about 1/4 mile of leisurely strolling through deep woods. You will find many of the typical forest flowers in this first gentle stretch, including twinflower, various huckleberries, one-sided wintergreen, pink wintergreen, coralroot, pipsissewa, vanilla leaf, foamflower, and dogwood. In small openings along the trail, slopes are thick with salal and Oregon-grape. Even if the green-leaf plants of the forest had no flowers, they would be fascinating just for the incredible variety of shapes, sizes, textures, and hues of their leaves.

Soon you will hear the roaring of Van Trump Creek, but before you cross it, you will walk across a short causeway over a spongy, mossy area where you will see masses of bog orchid, false lily-of-the-valley, bugbane, and devil's club. Just a few yards farther, you will cross a bridge over the spectacular cascades and pools of the creek.

From here you will begin the long, steady climb along the east side of the creek up to Comet Falls. You will switchback through woods, traverse across talus slopes, and cross occasional side creeks on your climb. In each of these special environments you will find wonderful wildflowers.

In the woods, in addition to more of the flowers you saw along the first 1/4 mile, look for rattlesnake plantain, ram's-horn pedicularis, twayblade, dwarf bramble, arnica, and strawberry bramble. On the open hillsides and along avalanche paths, expect white rhododendron, salmonberry, thimbleberry, goatsbeard, paintbrush, spiraea, elderberry, mountain ash, bluebells, leafy aster, tall penstemon, columbine, selfheal, pearly everlasting, valerian, edible thistle, and orange agoseris. In seep areas and places where creeks cross the trail, you will probably see bog orchid, yellow monkeyflower, cow parsnip, tiger lily, yellow willow-herb, spring beauty, fringecup, brook saxifrage, mitrewort, veronica, corn lily, and shooting star.

After about 1.75 miles, you will come to a branch of Van Trump Creek. From the bridge across it, you can look up the creek to the small but showy and energetic falls of mist and spray. As wonderful as this waterfall is, just a few more steps will bring you to the gorgeous Comet Falls—320' of gossamer comet tail falling softly to earth. If it's a hot day, you may enjoy standing in the spray near its base, but be **careful** not to slip on the wet rocks.

Trail descending from Van Trump Park

Then, if you choose, you may climb the comet's tail as the trail switchbacks steeply up out of the woods and into the glorious subalpine meadows of Van Trump Park, just below the icy flanks of Mt. Rainier's frozen dome.

For the next mile or so after Comet Falls, you will climb about 1000', traversing dense fields of subalpine flowers, many of which are described in the subalpine section (and can also be found at Paradise). Look for such flowers as magenta paintbrush, avalanche lily, bracted lousewort, subalpine lupine, beargrass, red heather, cinquefoil, veronica, blue violet, bird's-beak lousewort, phlox, leafy aster, white heather, and pasqueflower.

When you finally reach the end of the trail, high on a knoll amid some of Rainier's most gorgeous, green subalpine meadows, the mountain splendor (and your climb) will take your breath away! Wildflowers will surround you while snowfields and waterfalls will be just a short distance away; Mt. Adams and the now truncated Mt. St. Helens will loom on the horizon, while the glistening summit of Mt. Rainier will tower above you.

From here you can truly appreciate the elevational zones of Rainier, for in the last few hours you will have climbed through the forest zone and into the subalpine zone, and the alpine zone will be within sight just above you.

Van Trump Park

Closed & Open Canopy

With all the rain, rich soil, and deep forests in Rainier, the conditions are ideal for a vast and varied population of parasites and saprophytes. Rainier's forests boast all sorts of fungi and numerous species of strange flowering plants without green leaves that thrive in the deep forest duff by feeding off the living or the decaying tissue of other plants for nutrients.

In addition to these various non-green plants, the extensive forests of Rainier are also home to many species of flowering green-leaf plants that do photosynthesize for a living. Because these green-leaf plants need sunlight to fuel their food-making, they tend to grow in lighter or open areas of the woods where more sunlight gets through for at least part of the day. Look for these green-leaf plants in small forest openings and along the edges of trails. Although you may occasionally find some of these plants in what appears to be deep shade, they will probably be lit up by the sun at another time of day as the sun shifts and penetrates the canopy.

33

Most of the flowers you will encounter in these deep closed canopy and open canopy forest environments are greenish white or white, light yellow, or pale pink. Although many families are represented in these environments, the heath family is especially prevalent with many species of both saprophytes and green-leaf plants, both herbs and shrubs.

Along the featured trail and elsewhere: On our featured hike to Comet Falls and Van Trump Park, you will find most of the closed canopy forest and open canopy forest plants included in this book along the trail (or within easy view from it) as it winds through the woods. Although you will find some of these plants in the forested parts of the trail above Comet Falls (up to about 5000'), they will be much more plentiful in the lower parts of the trail in the 1.9 miles between the trailhead and the falls (3600–4800').

A few of the closed canopy forest and open canopy forest plants described here probably won't be found on the Comet Falls Trail. In these cases I have indicated another Rainier forest location where you can find them. Hike any of the numerous forest trails in Rainier and you will probably find most of the flowers described here. Just look in the relatively dry areas of the forest (flowers of wet areas are described in the next section).

Causeway along Comet Falls Trail

Trillium ovatum

Western Trillium

The leaves of trillium are nearly as beautiful and showy as the flowers. They are long (to 6") and broad, distinctly parallel-veined, and **occur in a whorl of 3 that neatly mimics the 3-petaled flowers**. • The theme of 3 continues with trillium: above the whorl of 3 leaves and just below the 3 large (1–2"), tongue-like, white petals are 3 green, leaf-like sepals that are rotated to show between the petals. Only 1 flower sits atop each stalk, which may grow up to 1½' tall. • As a final artistic touch on this gorgeous plant, the bright white petals turn an elegant purple or pink with age (see lower photo).

Typical location: woods, e.g., along lower part of trail to Comet Falls (3600–4000').

Distribution: below 6000'— Cascades and coastal mountains from southern British Columbia to northern California; Sierra Nevada (very uncommon); Rockies from Colorado north.

Names: *Trillium* refers to the 3 leaves, 3 sepals, 3 petals, and 3 stigmas. *Ovatum*, meaning 'oval,' refers to the broad leaves. Also known as wake-robin, which refers to the early blooming, at just about the time the robins 'wake' to announce spring.

- ■ **white (fading purple)**
- ● **3 separate petals**
- ✿ **May–July**

LILY FAMILY

Clintonia uniflora

Queen's Cup

Typical location: forests and small forest openings—upper forest zone, e.g., along trail to Comet Falls (4000–4800').

Distribution: 3000–6000'— Cascades and coastal mountains from Alaska to northern California; Sierra Nevada; Montana.

Names: Dewitt Clinton was a botanist and a governor of New York in the early 1800s. *Uniflora* means 'one flower.' Also known as bride's bonnet or beadlily. The less commonly used name, beadlily, refers to the bead-like berry.

■ white
● 6 separate tepals
✿ May–July

The name queen's cup is a deserving title for this elegant and striking plant. The flowers are large (1–1½" across) and showy, and their bright white, open bowls stand out dramatically from the forest floor. • Each flower sits alone atop the 2–6" plant stem that rises out of a pair (sometimes a trio) of 3–8" tongue-like, basal leaves. The arching leaves sometimes reach higher than the solitary flower. A single flower is dazzling with its **6 bright white tepals** (petals and sepals all alike), but the large showy clusters formed by creeping rhizomes create an even more spectacular display. • Out of the flower bowl rise 6 cylindrical, golden yellow stamens. When the flower goes to seed, the ovary becomes a single, bead-like, deep blue berry.

Streptopus amplexifolius   **3/6 PETALS • WHITE**

Clasping Twisted Stalk

The flowers of clasping twisted stalk are charming, but the leaves and stems (plant stems and flower stems) are more distinctive and intriguing. • The pointed, oval leaves clasp the stem at their base—the **slender stem often appears to pierce right through the base of the leaves**. The stem **zig-zags** back and forth from leaf to leaf, looking as though someone with needle and thread has strung the leaves on the plant. • The 1–3' plant is multi-branched and bears several of the ½" greenish-white flowers that dangle like bells. The 3 petals and 3 petal-like sepals flare out and back at the tips. The elongated fruits are ½" wide red or yellow berries (which sometimes turn dark purple).

Typical location: woods, e.g., along trail to Comet Falls (3600–4500').

Distribution: from 1000–5000'— Cascades and coastal mountains from Alaska to northern California; central North America.

Names: *Streptopus* means 'twisted foot,' probably in reference to the kinked flower stalks. *Amplexifolius*, meaning 'surround leaf,' describes the clasping leaves. The unique zig-zagged stem or the sharp bend in the flower stalks could be the origin of the name 'twisted stalk.'

■ **greenish white**
● **6 separate tepals**
✿ **June–July**

LILY FAMILY   *37*

Disporum hookeri

Hooker's Fairybell

Typical location: openings in woods, e.g., along Westside Road (2200'). Also found in subalpine parkland zone.

Distribution: below 5500'—Cascades and coastal mountains from Canada to California; Sierra Nevada.

Names: *Disporum* means 'double seed.' William Hooker was a 19th-century English botanist and botanical editor.

■ white
● 6 separate tepals
✿ May–July

Rainier forest trails seem to have a touch of mystery to them. The spongy floor underfoot, the primordial stillness, the lush leaves and exotic flowers, and the dim and mottled light all add to the mystic mood. Walking through these deep forests you almost expect some mythical creature to pop out from behind the next tree, so you're probably not at all surprised to come upon Hooker's fairybell. • Fairybell is perfectly named; the **dangling white flowers with the long, protruding stamens** have a delicate, airy, mischievous personality to them. The plant can grow up to 3' tall and is thick with broad leaves that often spread parallel to the ground, forming a canopy under which the impish flowers partly conceal themselves.

Listera cordata

Heart-leaved Twayblade

As with all orchids, twayblade's flowers have 5 similar perianth parts (2 petals and 3 sepals) and 1 part (petal) that is different. In heart-leaved twayblade, this characteristic is most apparent on close inspection. Unlike many orchids where the 6th part is much larger and/or dramatically different in color than the other 5, here the 6th part (**the lower lip of the flower**) is the same color and roughly the same size but quite a different shape: it **is forked into 2 prongs**, whereas the other 5 parts are elliptic and undivided.

• Though the flowers are not large or showy and the plant is not very tall (3–8"), as with many of the forest dwellers the leaves are distinctive and intriguing. Broad (1–1½" long and almost as wide) and somewhat heart-shaped leaves occur in only **1 opposite pair about halfway up the plant** stalk. • **Related plant:** Northwest twayblade (*L. caurina*) has pointier, egg-shaped leaves and has flowers with undivided spoon-shaped lower lips.

Typical location: both twayblades grow in woods, e.g., along trail to Comet Falls (3600–4500').

Distribution: 300–5000'— Cascades and coastal mountains from Alaska to northern California (where it is rare); eastern North America.

Names: M. Lister was an English naturalist of the 17th and early 18th centuries. *Cordata* means 'heart-shaped.' The common name, twayblade, refers to the pairs of opposite leaves.

■ **white**
● **3 petals and 3 sepals**
✿ **May–August**

Goodyera oblongifolia

Rattlesnake Plantain

Rattlesnake plantain has interesting, intricate flowers and eye-catching evergreen foliage. The 1–3" tongue-like leaves are dark green and leathery, forming thick clusters flat on the ground. The most striking characteristic of the leaves is their markings—a **central white stripe or often white mottling that resembles a rattlesnake's skin** (see lower photo). • Rising above its basal leaves is a solitary, slender ½–1½' stalk that bears (along its upper half) many of the small, greenish-white flowers in a narrow raceme. The upper sepal and upper 2 petals form a hood over the lower lip (the lower petal); the lateral 2 sepals bend outward. The resulting tubular, snout-like flowers tend to all face in the same direction, creating a mostly 1-sided flowering stem.

Typical location: woods, e.g., along lower part of trail to Comet Falls (3600–4000').

Distribution: 1500–7000'—Cascades and coastal mountains from southern Alaska to northern California; northern and central Sierra Nevada; eastern North America.

Names: John Goodyer was a 17th-century English botanist. *Oblongifolia* means 'oblong-leaved.' The common name, plantain, is in reference to the similarity of the leaves to those of plantain (*Plantago major* in the plantain family).

■ white
● 3 petals and 3 sepals
✿ July–August

Cornus canadensis | **4 PETALS • WHITE**

Canadian Dogwood

Dogwoods are a bit deceptive, for what appear to be large (½"), white petals in a cross are actually petal-like bracts that surround the true flowers—a central cluster of very small, greenish-white (or sometimes yellow or purplish) sepals, petals, and stamens. • Canadian dogwood's leaves are as striking and interesting as its flowers. The leaves are up to 3" long, broadly oval, and very distinctively and deeply veined. **They are arranged in whorls of 4–7 matching the cross-like pattern of the 4 large, white bracts.** • Because the plant spreads by underground runners (i.e., rhizomes), it usually occurs in profuse populations, dazzling us with numerous 'flowers' scattered atop a dense platform of leaves. • When dogwood goes to seed, the bright red berries are almost as showy as were the radiant white 'flowers.'

Typical location: woods, e.g., along lower part of trail to Comet Falls (3600–3800').

Distribution: below 4000'— Cascades and coastal mountains from Alaska to northern California; Rockies; eastern North America.

Names: *Cornus* means 'horn' in reference to its hard wood. *Canadensis* means 'of Canada.' Also known as bunchberry, which refers to the clusters of bright red fruits.

■ **white (bracts)**
● **4 petal-like bracts surrounding a cluster of tiny greenish-white flowers**
✿ **May–August**

DOGWOOD FAMILY

WHITE • 5 PETALS *Monotropa uniflora*

Single-flowered Indian Pipe

This strange **waxy-white plant** haunts the deep forests like a ghost, a ghost all the more ominous because it 'feeds' on its neighbors. Indian pipe is one of the many non-green saprophytes of Rainier forests. The 2–12" white stem bears a single ½–¾" white, nodding flower. The plants usually occur in large clusters, creating a pale, miniature forest whose contrast to the lush, dark green of the forest floor is startling and dramatic. • The stem of Indian pipe bears several narrow, almost transparent white bracts along its length, adding to its mysterious, spectral presence. • Typical of the heaths with nodding flowers, Indian pipe goes to seed as the stems become erect, holding the fruit upright. Later in the cycle, the plant tends to dry black.

Typical location: rich humus in woods, e.g., deep forest near Nickel Creek along trail from Steven's Canyon Road (3800'). **Uncommon in Rainier**.

Distribution: below 5000'—Cascades and coastal mountains from British Columbia to northern California (where it is rare); eastern North America.

Names: *Monotropa* means '1 direction' in reference to the flower nodding off to 1 side. *Uniflora* (see p. 36). The common name, Indian pipe, acknowledges this plant's resemblance to a ceremonial pipe.

- white
- 5 separate petals forming a nodding bell
- July–August

Allotropa virgata **5 PETALS • WHITE**

Candystick

Candystick is another of the many peculiar non-green saprophytes of the deep forest (most of which belong to the heath family). It is taller (6–18") and more varied in color than most of the others—the tall, thick, **white stems have flamboyant red (or maroon) stripes** spanning almost their entire length. • The small, white, urn-shaped flowers are crowded together in a dense spike covering most of the length of the stem; the 5 petals cradle 10 very conspicuous, dark red stamens. (Some botanists say that the petals are actually sepals.) Candystick is less common than most of the other saprophytic heaths, so consider yourself lucky if you see it.

Typical location: rich humus in woods, e.g., Cougar Rock Campground (3000'). **Uncommon in Rainier.**

Distribution: 200–9000'—Cascades and coastal mountains from southern British Columbia to northern California; Sierra Nevada (uncommon); Rockies in Montana.

Names: *Allotropa* means 'other turn' in reference to the changing orientation of the flowers: they turn upward when young, downward when older. *Virgata* means 'striped.' The common name, candystick, refers to the red-on-white plant stalk that will probably remind you of those sticky Christmas candy canes.

- ▦ white
- ● **5 separate petals forming an urn**
- ✿ **July–August**

WHITE • 5 PETALS   *Gaultheria shallon*

Salal

Typical location: forest edges, e.g., along lower parts of trail to Comet Falls (3600–4000').

Distribution: common and widespread below 4000'— Cascades and coastal mountains from Alaska to northern California; southern California coast.

Names: J.F. Gaulthier was an 18th-century Canadian botanist and physicist. *Shallon* is a Native American name.

▩ white
● 5 petals forming a hanging urn
✿ May–July

Salal is a very **common shrub** of the Rainier forests, prevalent along trails and on partially open slopes where some direct sun gets through. The **leaves are broad, shiny, and leathery**; the stems are wiry and tough. Although salal will usually form a dense shrub about knee-high, it sometimes grows to almost 6' and can form nearly impenetrable thickets.
• The flowers are the typical hanging urns of the heath family, though they are a bit larger than most. Several (5–15) of the ½" white flowers hang from the ends of each branch; the **reddish-blue to dark purple (almost black) berries** are juicy and quite edible.

Moneses uniflora — 5 PETALS • WHITE

Woodnymph

Woodnymph is one of the many plants of Rainier's deep forests with evergreen leaves and nodding, bell- or crown-shaped flowers. Formerly in the wintergreen family, botanists have put these plants into the heath family with heathers, huckleberries, azaleas, rhododendrons, and many of the non-green saprophytes. • Woodnymph is a small (less than 6" tall) but striking plant. Its **1 large (½–1" across), bright white flower nods almost face down** from the tip of its typically bare stem. The oval, toothed leaves are usually basal. • The flower face is a wonderful, delicate palette of colors and shapes. Five pairs of bright yellow, finger-like anthers lie flat against the white, waxy petals while out of the round, green ovary projects a straight, thick, cylindrical style with a disk-like stigma.

Typical location: deep forests or small openings in woods, e.g., Rain Forest Loop Trail at Carbon River (1900').

Distribution: 300–5000'— Cascades and coastal mountains from Alaska to northern California; central Sierra Nevada; across Canada and the northern U.S.

Names: *Moneses* means 'one delight'—as indeed is the solitary, crown-like flower. *Uniflora* (see p. 36). Also known as single delight. Formerly called *Pyrola uniflora*.

- white (pinkish)
- 5 petals forming a nodding crown
- May–July

HEATH FAMILY

One-sided Wintergreen

Typical location: woods, e.g., common along trail to Comet Falls (3600–4800').

Distribution: 3000–9000'— Cascades and coastal mountains from Alaska to northern California; Sierra Nevada; across Canada and northern U.S.

Names: *Orthilia* means 'straight spiral'—a rather cryptic reference to the 1-sided raceme. *Secunda* is from *secund*, which means 1-sided. Formerly called *Pyrola secunda*.

▦ **greenish white**
● **5 separate petals forming a nodding bell**
✿ **June–August**

One-sided wintergreen is the most common of Rainier's many wintergreens (i.e., genera *Pyrola*, *Orthilia*, *Chimaphila*, and *Moneses*, all of which are now members of the heath family). It is probably the least showy of these plants with inconspicuous (very small and greenish-white) flowers and non-distinctive leaves (not veined like those of *Pyrola picta* or purple-backed like those of *P. asarifolia*, p. 60). However, one-sided wintergreen's unique feature is its **4–20 bell-shaped flowers that nod off the same side of the stem**. • Some of the oval leaves are basal, while others branch off the lower part of the 2–8" stem. They are shiny, conspicuously scalloped or toothed, and evergreen. • The style protrudes well beyond the 5 petals and is straight (unlike the curving or bent style of many of the other wintergreens).

Arctostaphylos uva-ursi   **5 PETALS • WHITE**

Kinnikinnick

Kinnikinnick is a charming little **prostrate shrub** that usually grows less than a foot tall but often forms extensive, dense mats. The 1" ovate, evergreen leaves are leathery and shiny, providing a pleasing contrast to the **reddish bark** and the delicate, white to pink blossoms. • The flowers are typical of the heath family; the **hanging urns with tips that resemble puckered kisses** are easily recognizable as being of the manzanita (*Arctostaphylos*) genus. • The berries (little red 'apples') persist on the plant into the winter, providing valuable food for bears and other animals at a time when most berries are long gone.

Typical location: forest edges and openings, rocky outcrops, e.g., along lower parts of Eagle Peak Trail out of Longmire (2700'). Also found in subalpine parkland zone.

Distribution: below 10,000'— Cascades and coastal mountains from Alaska to California; Sierra Nevada; Rockies; across Canada and northern U.S.

Names: Both the genus name *Arctostaphylos* and the species name *uva-ursi* mean 'bear's grapes' in reference to the late persisting berries. Also known as bearberry. Kinnikinnick is a Native American word for a tobacco-like mixture.

■ white (pink)
● 5 petals forming a
   hanging urn
✿ May–June

Foamflower

Foamflower is one of the most delicate plants of Rainier's forests: its **tiny, white flowers dance on their slender stalks** like flecks of sea foam being blown by the wind. The narrow (thread-like) petals and the long-protruding, whisker-like stamens contribute greatly to the airy, fragile look of the flowers. • Many of the ⅛–¼", pale white flowers branch off the slender stalk that rises ½–1½' above the long-stalked, basal leaves (there are also a few smaller stem leaves). The basal leaves are broad and thin with sharply toothed edges and are 3–5 lobed (somewhat maple-like) or are divided into 3 leaflets. • When foamflower goes to seed, its seed capsules split to form 'sugar scoops' (see Names below) ready to dish out the many small, shiny black seeds within. • You may occasionally find solitary plants, but you will usually find this plant growing in clusters, spreading its 'foam' over large patches of ground.

Typical location: moist edges of woods, e.g., common along trail to Comet Falls (3600–4800').

Distribution: below 8000'—Cascades and coastal mountains from Alaska to northern California.

Names: *Tiarella* means 'small tiara,' apparently in reference to the appearance of the flowers. *Trifoliata* means '3 leaf' in reference to the 3 leaflets of 1 variety. Also known as sugar scoop.

- white
- 5 separate petals
- May–August

SAXIFRAGE FAMILY

Rubus lasiococcus | **5 PETALS • WHITE**

Creeping Raspberry

Creeping raspberry has a very attractive white flower, but it is the fruit—a cluster of **tasty, red raspberry-like drupelets**—that is most appealing. • Creeping raspberry is indeed a low plant with a creeping runner that roots every now and then at its nodes. The leaves are broad, rough, toothed, and 3-lobed. The flowers are solitary on 5–8" stems and are typical of the rose family with 5 broad, separate petals surrounding a cluster of many reproductive parts. Creeping raspberry is unusual for a rose family member in that it is unisexual, i.e., flowers with only stamens grow on some plants, while flowers with only pistils grow on others. • This bramble is a friendly one—no prickles.

Typical location: forest edges—upper forest zone, e.g., upper parts of trail to Comet Falls (4000–4800').

Distribution: 3500–6500'—Cascades and coastal mountains from southern British Columbia to northern California.

Names: *Rubus* is the Latin name for bramble. *Lasiococcus* means 'hairy berry,' which is certainly an accurate description of the densely hairy fruit. Also known as dwarf bramble.

▨ **white**
● **5 separate petals**
✿ **June–August**

Fragaria vesca

Wild Strawberry

Typical location: forest openings, e.g., along Westside Road (2200'). Also found in subalpine parkland zone.

Distribution: 100–6000'— Cascades and coastal mountains from Alaska to California; Sierra Nevada; Rockies; eastern North America.

Names: *Fragaria* means 'fragrant.' *Vesca* means 'weak.' The common name, strawberry, may be in reference to a practice of placing straw around domestic plants to protect the berries from getting muddy in wet weather.

With strawberries, raspberries, and brambles, the forest floor is thick with white, 5-petaled, rose-like flowers and delicious, juicy berries. All of these plants spread by runners and have rather similar lobed, toothed, and deeply veined leaves. • Wild strawberry has 3-lobed **leaves that are smoother on the surface** than those of the brambles and raspberries, though their edges are jagged with sawtooth teeth. The ½–¾" bright white flowers perch atop stems that rise only a few inches above the reddish runners. • Unlike some of its relatives, wild strawberry's reproductive parts are yellow, providing a striking contrast to the white petals. • The **berry is red and delicious**!

■ white
● **5 separate petals**
✿ **May–July**

Oplopanax horridum **5 PETALS • WHITE**

Devil's Club

Devil's club is truly *horridum*: the nightmare images conjured up by its names are matched by reality! Watch out for this monster when hiking—it is armed and dangerous. • The thick stem that frequently reaches 6' (and sometimes 10') and the huge, maple-like leaves (up to 1' across) are both **heavily armed with barbed spines** that can pierce and tear and, even worse, stick and fester. In spite of, or perhaps because of, its forbidding appearance, devil's club was considered by various Native American groups to be an important guardian and benefactor, capable of warding off evil spirits and treating various ailments. • The small, greenish-white flowers are packed into a large (to 5") cone-shaped cluster that grows out of a leaf axil. The berries are bright red.

Typical location: moist areas in woods, e.g., along lower part of trail to Comet Falls (3600–3800').

Distribution: below 4000'—Cascades and coastal mountains from Alaska to Oregon.

Names: *Oploanax* means 'armed healer' in reference to its paradoxical nature as assailant and curative. The meaning of *horridum* can be seen and felt.

■ **greenish white**
● **5 separate petals**
✿ **June–July**

Achlys triphylla

Vanilla Leaf

Typical location: woods, e.g., along lower part of trail to Comet Falls (3600–4500').

Distribution: below 5000'— Cascades and coastal mountains from southern British Columbia to northern California.

Names: *Achlys* means 'mist' or 'obscure.' These plants usually grow in tight masses with the broad leaves forming an uninterrupted carpet above which floats the 'mist' of small, white flowers. The name could also refer to this plant's deep forest (obscure) environment. *Triphylla* refers to the 3-part leaves.

■ white
● no petals or sepals
  (cluster of stamens)
✿ May–July

Leaves, leaves, and more leaves. One of the most intriguing and prevalent leaves in the low- to mid-elevation woods is that of vanilla leaf. Its **large, 3-parted foliage is reminiscent of a moose head complete with antlers**! • Many of the 4–12" leaf-bearing petioles can sprout up from a single rhizome, causing vanilla leaf to occur in great masses, creating a nearly solid canopy over a large area of forest floor. The white flowers are very small and grow in a ½–2" spike on a tall, leafless stalk that reaches up above the leaves. The flowers actually have no petals or sepals but consist of 8–20 long, delicate reproductive parts.

BARBERRY FAMILY

Adenocaulon bicolor   **NO/MANY PETALS • WHITE**

Pathfinder

Though pathfinder has only small, inconspicuous flowers, it is nevertheless a distinctive plant for its height, its somewhat puzzling flowers, and its vibrant leaves. • The very slender, branching stem may rise up to 3' above the 4–12" basal leaves that are broadly triangular or heart-shaped. When the leaves are turned over by the brush of a foot, their **white-wooly undersides** can create a bright path back out of the forest. • Many of the tiny (⅛") white inflorescences sit on the tips of the branches. Pathfinder has only disk flowers, a few of which are pistillate (female)—these are the 5-petaled and tubular flowers—and the rest of which are staminate (male) without corolla tubes.

Typical location: small openings in woods—lower forest zone, e.g., along Grove of the Patriarchs Trail (2200').

Distribution: below 6500'—Cascades and coastal mountains from southern British Columbia to northern California; Sierra Nevada.

Names: *Adenocaulon* means 'gland stem' in reference to the stalked glands that cover the upper part of the stem. *Bicolor* refers to the 2-colored leaves that are green above and white below. Also known as trail plant.

▪ white
● few disk flowers in a small head
✿ July–August

Berberis nervosa

Cascade Oregon-grape

Typical location: openings in woods, e.g., along lower part of trail to Comet Falls (3600–4000').

Distribution: below 6000'— Cascades and coastal mountains from southern British Columbia to northern California; northern Sierra Nevada (uncommon).

Names: *Berberis* is the Arabic name for barberry. *Nervosa* means 'nerved' in reference to the veining on the leaves. Also known as *Mahonia nervosa*. The common name, Oregon-grape, refers to the blue-purple grape-like fruits, which, though edible, should not be eaten in large quantities.

- yellow
- 6 petals in 2 whorls of 3
- May–June

Oregon-grape is a low (to 2'), evergreen shrub whose leaves add wonderful patterns and textures to the mosaic of forest greenery. Its reddish leaf stems each bear 4–9 opposite pairs of leaflets plus 1 terminal leaflet, all of which **resemble holly leaves— shiny, leathery, and toothed**.
- The **bright yellow flowers** grow in dense, narrow, erect clusters that may reach 8" long. The cluster of blue to purple berries are very attractive and tasty (tart); some people mix them with sweeter berries of other plants (e.g., salal, p. 44) to make a unique-tasting jelly. • On close inspection, you will find the flowers rather odd, for they have 9 sepals in 3 whorls of 3, and 6 petals in 2 whorls of 3.

BARBERRY FAMILY

Monotropa hypopitys

Pine-sap

Next to western coralroot (p. 57), pine-sap is probably the most common of the deep forest saprophytes. Though common, it is nonetheless quite striking with its **pale yellow or orangish-yellow (sometimes pinkish) flowers and stems and the distinctive 1-sided nod of the flowers**. • The fleshy stem, which may reach 10", bears several small, almost transparent, scale-like, non-green 'leaves' along its length. The tip of the stem curls sharply over to 1 side and bears a cluster of several to many ½" bell-shaped flowers. • When the plant first emerges from the soil, the tip of the stem bearing the flowers is already nodding; much later, when the flowers go to seed, the stem becomes erect. Later still, the plant dries black.

Typical location: rich humus in deep woods, e.g., along lower part of trail to Comet Falls (3600–3800').

Distribution: 350–7000'—Cascades and coastal mountains from southern Alaska to northern California; eastern U.S.

Names: *Monotropa* (see p. 42). *Hypopitys* means 'beneath pine trees' in reference to its habitat. Also known as many-flowered Indian pipe. In some books this plant is called *Hypopitys monotropa*. The common name, pine-sap, could be in reference to the resemblance of the flower to the sap of a pine tree, or it could be pointing to the plant's habit of growing under pines (and other conifers) and 'sapping' their strength.

■ yellow (pinkish)
● 5 separate petals forming a nodding bell
❀ June–August

HEATH FAMILY

**YELLOW/ORANGE
5 PETALS**

Pleuricospora fimbriolata

Fringed Pine-sap

Fringed pine-sap resembles its fellow heath and close relative pine-sap (*Monotropa hypopitys*, p. 55) in several ways, but it is different enough to be placed in a separate genus. • Both species are non-green, forest sapro-phytes; both are heaths and so have urn-shaped or bell-shaped flowers; and both are called pine-sap, probably because of the color and texture of their flowers (fleshy orangish yellow or creamy yellow bearing some resemblance to the sap of pine trees). However, the stem of fringed pine-sap is erect (not nodding) and barely emerges from the soil, so the **dense clusters of erect ½" flowers rest almost directly on the ground**. • At first glance, you might not even realize that fringed pine-sap has flowers. You might think it is a non-flowering fungus, but on closer examination you will see that the yellow head actually consists primarily of many small, tubular flowers crowded tightly together. • The 4 or 5 petals are often jagged on the edges. Down inside the flower is a broad, crown-like, yellow stigma somewhat resembling a puckered mouth. This plant is not only bizarre, it's downright ominous-looking!

Typical location: rich humus of deep woods, e.g., in deep forest near Nickel Creek on trail off Steven's Canyon Road (3800'). **Uncommon in Rainier**.

Distribution: 500–9000'—Cascades and coastal mountains from British Columbia to northern California (uncommon); Sierra Nevada (uncommon).

Names: *Pleuricospora* means 'seeds at the side.' *Fimbriolata* means 'fringed' in reference to the petals.

- yellow to cream
- 4 or 5 separate petals forming an urn
- ✿ June–July

HEATH FAMILY

Corallorhiza mertensiana | **3/6 PETALS • PINK/RED**

Western Coralroot

Although very common in the deep forests, western coralroot never fails to delight. • Though it has no green leaves (it is a saprophyte feeding off decomposing forest litter), more often than not you will find a thick cluster of these plants beautifully spotlighted in a shaft of light beaming through an opening in the woods. • Branching off the top half or so of the ½–1½' reddish stem are several of the graceful, somewhat **fragile-looking pink or reddish flowers**. Of the 6 perianth parts typical of orchids, the 3 sepals and the 2 lateral petals are all quite similar—slender, ¼–½" long, and pink to red (sometimes with dark red or yellow veins). The 6th part of the perianth (i.e., the 3rd petal), which forms the lower lip of the flower is **somewhat broader, usually deeper pink with 3 dark red veins, and often white-tipped**. • The bright yellow column housing the reproductive parts arches over and contrasts sharply with the rich pink lower lip.

Typical location: rich humus in woods (often in sunny spots), e.g., along trail to Comet Falls (3600–4500').

Distribution: below 7000'—Cascades and coastal mountains from southern Alaska to northern California; Rockies from Wyoming north.

Names: The genus name *Corallorhiza* and the common name coralroot both refer to this plant's roots resembling coral. Also known as Merten's coralroot after F.C. Mertens, a German botanist of the late 18th and early 19th centuries.

■ pink
● 3 petals and 3 sepals
✿ June–July

Calypso bulbosa

Fairy Slipper

Though only 6" tall and inhabiting the semi-dark of deep forest, fairy slipper is one of the most spectacular of Rainier's wildflowers. It certainly does not dazzle by massive displays or sun-lit brilliance, but if you are lucky enough to find one it will captivate you with its beauty. • A single 1–1 ½" flower sits atop its short stem, though you may find 2 or 3 plants growing close together. Each plant has only 1 broad, egg-shaped 1–2" leaf, which is produced in the fall and persists through the winter but withers in summer. • The stunning flower consists of 5 similar, narrow, **rose-purple sepals and petals** flaring out and up, and, as with all orchids, 1 much different lower petal. In fairy slipper this **lower petal forms a broad, slipper-like pouch** that is white (or yellowish) with streaks and splotches of red or purple. This flower is a delight to the nose as well as to the eye, because it has a delicate, sweet fragrance.

Typical location: rich humus of deep woods, e.g., along trail paralleling the Nisqually River in Longmire area (2700'). **Uncommon in Rainier**.

Distribution: below 6000'—Cascades and coastal mountains from Alaska to northern California; Rockies; northeast North America.

Names: *Calypso* is after Kalypso, the beautiful and secretive sea nymph in Homer's Odyssey. *Bulbosa* refers to the plant's bulb-like corm. Also known as calypso orchid.

■ red-purple
● 3 petals and 3 sepals
✿ May–June

ORCHID FAMILY

Chimaphila umbellata | **5 PETALS • PINK/RED**

Pippsissewa

Pipsissewa, or prince's pine, is one of the most elegant of all the forest plants, whether in bloom or in bud. Its ½–1' stem bears an **'umbrella' of 3 or more of the nodding, pinkish flowers suspended from the ends of reddish, rather wiry-looking spokes** (i.e., pedicels).

• When the flowers are wide open in bloom with their 5 separate, downward-facing petals and 10 hanging stamens, they resemble graceful crowns; when they are in bud, they look a bit like hanging street lanterns (see lower photo). • Pipsissewa is an evergreen with whorls of shiny, leathery leaves that are usually sharply toothed, especially near the tips. The 1 or 2 whorls of leaves usually come off the bottom half of the stem, so several inches of bare stem (terminating in the flower umbels) rise above the leaves.

Typical location: woods, e.g., along trail to Comet Falls (3600–4500').

Distribution: 1000–9000'—Cascades and coastal mountains from British Columbia to northern California; Sierra Nevada; Rockies; eastern North America.

Names: *Chimaphila* means 'winter loving' in reference to its evergreen nature. *Umbellata* refers to the umbel of flowers branching off the top of the stalk. The common name, pipsissewa, is an Indian name meaning 'it breaks into small pieces' in reference to the leaves that presumably contain a substance that can dissolve kidney stones. Also known as western prince's pine.

■ pink
● 5 separate petals forming a nodding crown
✿ June–July

HEATH FAMILY

Pink Wintergreen

Typical location: woods, e.g., along lower part of trail to Comet Falls (3600–4000').

Distribution: 300–9000'— Cascades and coastal mountains from Alaska to northern California; Sierra Nevada; Rockies; eastern North America.

Names: *Pyrola* means 'little pear' in reference to the leaf shape. *Asarifolia* means 'asarum-leaved.' (*Asarum* is wild ginger that has shiny, dark green, heart-shaped leaves.) The common name, wintergreen, refers to the leaves' persistence through 1 winter, resulting in a plant with last year's and this year's leaves.

■ pink
● 5 separate petals forming a hanging cup
✿ June–August

Pink wintergreen is another of the graceful, green-leaf heaths of the forests (though you may also find it in open boggy areas). All the wintergreens (i.e., genera *Pyrola*, *Orthilia*, *Chimaphila*, and *Moneses*) were formerly considered to be members of their own wintergreen family, but they have been merged into the heath family. • The slender stem of pink wintergreen rises high (to 16") above the broad, shiny, dark green basal leaves. Sometimes the leaves are round, sometimes they are heart-shaped, often they are purplish on their undersides. • Many (8–25) of the ½", **waxy, pink to deep red, cup-shaped flowers hang downward** from their short pedicels. Out of the 5 petals protrudes a long, outward-curving style.

Vaccinium parviflorum

Red Huckleberry

Of all the many Rainier plants with delicious berries, the huckleberries (otherwise called blueberries) are the most common and, luckily for hikers and bears, among the tastiest. Along almost any forest trail in Rainier, regardless of elevation, you will encounter several species of huckleberries often forming dense thickets. In mid-summer, enjoy the beauty of the delicately hanging, pink or white, urn-shaped flowers (typical of the heath family). • Red huckleberry is a **shrub, up to 10' tall,** with bright green branches and small (1") ovate leaves. The flowers are small (¼") pinkish (sometimes white or yellowish) urns that turn to **bright red, rather tart and tasty berries.** • **Related plant:** Oval-leaf blueberry (*V. ovalifolium*) is a smaller shrub of 6' or so with larger, blunt leaves, pink flowers, and dusty blue-black berries (see lower photo).

Typical location: woods, e.g., common along trail to Comet Falls (3600–4500').

Distribution: below 5000'— Cascades and coastal mountains from Alaska to northern California; Sierra Nevada. Oval-leaf blueberry extends into subalpine elevations and doesn't reach as far south as California.

Names: *Vaccinium* is the ancient Latin name for this genus. *Parviflorum* means 'small-flowered.' The common name, huckleberry, comes from an Anglo-Saxon word meaning 'small plant.'

■ pink
● 5 petals forming a hanging urn
✿ June–July

HEATH FAMILY

Linnaea borealis

Twinflower

Typical location: small openings in woods, e.g., common along lower part of trail to Comet Falls (3600–4200').

Distribution: 750–8000'—Cascades and coastal mountains from Alaska to northern California; northern Sierra Nevada; Rockies; across Canada and northern U.S.

Names: Carolus Linnaeus was the Swedish naturalist who developed the binomial system of nomenclature (giving each organism a 2-word Latin name—genus and species). *Borealis* means 'northern,' as in aurora borealis, the northern lights.

■ pink
● 5 petals forming a nodding bell
✿ June–August

Twinflower has cute little flowers that **nod in romantic pairs** off the short (6") stalk. The plant's long runners, which trail across the forest duff, give rise to scores of flowering stems. In small clearings in the woods, you can often come across large colonies of these charming plants, each with its pair of flowers dancing just a few inches above the opposite pairs of basal, 1/2", shiny, leathery leaves. • The short plant stalk forks into a 'Y' at its apex; from the tip of each branch of this 'Y' hangs 1 of the **pink (white-tinged), 1/2–3/4", fringed, bell-shaped flowers**. The style (with stigma) protrudes out of the bell, resembling a clapper about to sound. These delightful flowers have a soft, delicious honeysuckle fragrance.

HONEYSUCKLE FAMILY

Trientalis latifolia

Pacific Starflower

Starflower has delicate, pale pink, gracefully symmetrical blossoms. Though the plant is only 4–10" tall, everything about it is eye-catching. The whorl of 4–8 broad leaves forms a perfect backdrop for the star-shaped flower. Each flower (often only 1, but sometimes several) is perched atop a very slender stem rising out of the center of the leaf whorl. • **The pointed petals overlap, forming an exquisite ½", pastel pink (sometimes white) star.** Usually it is a 6-pointed or 7-pointed star, but there can be as few as 5 petals or as many as 9.

Typical location: deep woods or small openings in woods, e.g., along Grove of the Patriarchs Trail (2200').

Distribution: below 5000'— Cascades and coastal mountains from southern British Columbia to northern California; Sierra Nevada; Idaho.

Names: *Trientalis* means 'about ⅓' in reference to its usual height (about ⅓'). *Latifolia* means 'broad-leaved.' Formerly called *T. borealis*.

■ pink (white)
● 5–9 petals fused at the base
✿ May–July

PRIMROSE FAMILY

Wet Areas

Though most of the lower elevations in Rainier are heavily forested, these forests are not completely homogeneous environments. There are several specialized habitats within the forests that are home to different associations of plants. In the previous subsection of this book we saw how deep forest habitats tend to harbor different plants than those found in the open canopy areas (e.g., borders of trails, small clearings) where a bit more direct sunlight gets in. Another specialized habitat within the forest environment is represented by the wet or soggy creekbanks, seep areas, and boggy flats. Any particularily wet area where the ground is soggy will provide different conditions and will house different plants than will the drier areas in the woods. Most of these wet areas will not be in deep shade, but will be in clearings where much more sunlight gets through.

Along the featured trail and elsewhere: Along the forest trail to Comet Falls, you will encounter several such wet areas: some areas are still within the forest shade, while others are in clearings with more sun exposure. In the first 1/4 mile, the trail, still in the thick forest, crosses a short causeway before reaching a bridge over Van Trump Creek.

This mini-marsh is a terrific place to see many of the flowers included in this section. (It goes without saying that you must stay on the causeway, because venturing into the bog could cause considerable damage to the plants.)

Farther along the trail, there are several places where the forest opens up and the trail is bordered by hillside seeps. Look here for most of the other flowers described in this section. You may also find a few of the plants included in this section growing in wet, open meadows above the thick forests.

Although there is a wide diversity of families and genera that inhabit these wet forest environments, the saxifrage family and the buttercup family seem to be the most abundantly represented. As you might expect of plants getting more sun and lots of water, most of these wet forest species have large, deep green leaves.

Saxifrage

WHITE • 3/6 PETALS *Smilacina racemosa*

Plumose False Solomon's Seal

Typical location: moist areas in woods, e.g., along Westside Road (2200'). Also found in subalpine zone.

Distribution: below 8000'— Cascades and coastal mountains from British Columbia to California; Sierra Nevada; Rockies; eastern North America.

Names: *Smilacina* means 'little *Smilax*,' another genus in the lily family. *Racemosa* means 'in a raceme.' The common name false Solomon's seal refers to a strange 'Star of David' marking seen on the stalk of a related plant.

The leaves of false Solomon's seal are among the most beautiful of the forest. They are large (up to 8"), gracefully elliptical, and deeply parallel-veined. • The ¼", creamy white flowers enhance the graceful appearance of the plant. In plumose false Solomon's seal they are **clustered in soft, branched plumes**. • The plant is tall (2–3') and tends to form dense 'thickets.' The berries are showy and edible, though not especially tasty.

• **Related plant:** Star-flowered false Solomon's seal (*S. stellata*) is a similar tall plant, but its white flowers occur in much looser, unbranched inflorescences of fewer flowers. The 2 false Solomon's seals occur in similar habitats and often grow together.

■ white
● 6 separate tepals
✿ May–July

Platanthera stricta   **3/6 PETALS • WHITE**

Slender Bog Orchid

S lender bog orchid is slender, and also subtle. **Its flowers are a soft green or greenish white** (an unusual color for a flower). Though the plant may grow to 3' tall, it may be hard to spot, because the flowers and the stem blend easily into their mostly green, wet environment. • **Many (5–30) of the waxy, ¼–½" flowers are crowded along the upper part of the stout stem.** Like other orchids, the flowers of slender bog orchid have 6 perianth parts (petals and sepals), 5 alike and 1 different. In slender bog orchid, the 6th part (the lower petal) is shorter than the other petals and sepals and is broad and sac-like. • Unlike most other orchids of the area that have only basal leaves, slender bog orchid has tongue-like leaves all the way up the stem. • This plant rewards close inspection; its intricate structure and delicate color are very satisfying and appealing.

Typical location: streambanks and boggy areas in woods—upper forest zone, e.g., in boggy flat along causeway near beginning of trail to Comet Falls (3600'). Also found in subalpine zone.

Distribution: 3000–7000'—Cascades and coastal mountains from Alaska to northern California; Rockies from Montana south.

Names: *Platanthera* means 'wide anther.' *Stricta* means 'constricted' or 'slender' in reference to the narrow terminal cluster of flowers (i.e., the flowers are tight to the stem). Also known as green bog orchid. Formerly called *Habenaria saccata*.

- ▨ **green (greenish white)**
- ● **3 petals and 3 sepals**
- ✿ **May–August**

ORCHID FAMILY

WHITE • 4 PETALS   *Maianthemum dilatatum*

False Lily-of-the-valley

Although false lily-of-the-valley has the parallel-veined leaves and the symmetrical flowers typical of the lily family, the flower has only 4 petal-like parts (rather than the 3 or 6 you would expect from a lily). • The 4–12" stem bears a spike-like raceme of tiny **white flowers, which have protruding stamens that create a fuzzy, spider-like appearance**. The fruits are round, shiny berries, starting green with brown mottling and later turning red (see lower photo). The leaves (1 or 2 to a plant) are this plant's most noticeable feature. They are large (2–4" long and 1–2" wide), shiny, heart-shaped, and distinctly parallel-veined. The plants often form large, dense clusters (they spread by rhizomes) that create a luscious, low canopy of shiny green over the forest floor.

Typical location: wet areas in openings in woods, e.g., in boggy flat along causeway near beginning of trail to Comet Falls (3600').

Distribution: below 4500'—Cascades and coastal mountains from Alaska to northern California; Idaho.

Names: *Maianthemum* means 'May flower' in reference to the flower's early blooming. *Dilatatum* means 'spread out,' perhaps in reference to splayed out 'petals' or perhaps to the spreading stamens. Also known as beadruby because of the small, round berries that somewhat resemble a string of beads.

■ white
● 4 petal-like sepals
✿ May–July

LILY FAMILY

Tellima grandiflora

Fringecup

Fringecup is a typically strange member of the saxifrage family. Its leaves are large (2–3" long and as broad), mostly basal, round or heart-shaped, shallowly lobed, and coarsely toothed. Its stalks are also typical of saxifrages—slender, mostly leafless, and bearing numerous flowers. In fringecup, 10–35 of the ½" cup-like flowers are arranged on a tall (1–3') spike. • The flowers are the unusual part of this plant: the sepals form a greenish cup, out of which flare the 5 widely separated, lobed petals. The petals begin whitish and age pink, brown, or even bright red. **The flower somewhat resembles a strange frog-like creature with 5 webbed feet!** The 10 anthers are bright orange.

Typical location: along streambanks and in seep areas in woods, e.g., on seepy slope in clearing along upper part of trail to Comet Falls (4200').

Distribution: below 6500'— Cascades and coastal mountains from Alaska to central California; northern Sierra Nevada; Rockies in Montana.

Names: *Tellima* is an anagram of *Mitella*, the genus name of another saxifrage (mitrewort, p. 70) whose strange, fringed petals bear some resemblance to the petals of fringecup. *Grandiflora* means 'large-flowered'—perhaps for a saxifrage!

■ white (aging reddish brown)
● 5 separate petals each with 5–7 lobes
✿ May–July

SAXIFRAGE FAMILY

Mitella breweri

Brewer's Mitrewort

Typical location: along streambanks and in seep areas in forest clearings—upper forest zone, e.g., on seepy slope in clearing along upper part of trail to Comet Falls (4200'). Also found in subalpine zone.

Distribution: 3500–11,000'—Cascades and coastal mountains from southern British Columbia to northern California; Sierra Nevada.

Names: *Mitella* means 'small capsule' in reference to the fruits. William Brewer worked on California botany in the late 1800s and on the U.S. Geological Survey (USGS)/Whitney survey of California from 1860–64.

- greenish
- 5 separate petals each with 'antennae'
- May–August

B rewer's mitrewort is another odd saxifrage. It has the broad basal leaves you associate with wet-environment saxifrages; however, unlike many of its kin, mitrewort's leaves are only shallowly lobed and barely toothed (rounded teeth, not sharp ones). The 1–4" roundish or kidney-shaped leaves are shorter than they are wide. • The slender 4–16" stalk rising above the leaves bears many (20–60) of the peculiar, greenish flowers packed along the upper half or so of its length, looking like the **stalk is swarming with small, greenish spiders**. Use a magnifying glass and you will see that these bizarre ¼–½" flowers consist of a tiny pentagon saucer out of which flare 5 antenna-like petals, each with several thread-like appendages branching off the main axis. The 5 stamens alternate with the 5 petals. • When this plant goes to seed, the saucer overflows with hundreds of tiny, black seeds.

Saxifraga odontoloma   **5 PETALS • WHITE**

Brook Saxifrage

In a family known for its distinctive leaves, brook saxifrage may have the most striking and beautiful leaves of all. They are **broadly heart-shaped (1–2" across) with a conspicuous U-shaped notch at the base where the petiole joins the leaf**, and the entire leaf (except for the notch) has edges with **sharp, triangular teeth**. When several plants grow close together, as is often the case, the leaves can form an almost solid ground cover, looking like a dense swarm of delicate, green butterflies drinking from the wet ground. • Rising above the basal leaves is a slender ½–1½' branching stem bearing many tiny (⅛–¼"), white flowers. The 5 flaring, spoon-shaped petals alternate with the narrow, club-shaped stamens; the sepals underneath are reflexed. With its petals, sepals, stamens, and pistil going in all different directions, the tiny flower has a rather frayed or airy look.

Typical location: along streambanks and in seep areas in forest clearings— upper forest zone, e.g., in seep area in clearing along upper part of trail to Comet Falls (4200'). Also found in subalpine zone.

Distribution: 3000–10,000'— Cascades and coastal mountains from Alaska to northern California; Sierra Nevada; Rockies.

Names: *Saxifraga* means 'rock-breaking' in reference to the rock habitat of some species. *Odontoloma* means 'tufted' in reference to the leaves. Formerly called *S. punctata*.

▪ **white**
● **5 separate petals**
✿ **June–August**

False Bugbane

Typical location: along streams and in boggy areas in woods, e.g., in boggy flat along causeway on lower part of trail to Comet Falls (3600').

Distribution: 3000–6000'— Cascades and coastal mountains from southern British Columbia to northern California; Sierra Nevada; Rockies.

Names: E.R. von Trautvetter was a 19th-century Russian botanist. *Caroliniensis* means 'of Carolina.' The common name false bugbane points to this plant's resemblance to the true bugbane (*Cimicifuga elata*), which has a very unpleasant insect-repelling odor.

■ white
● no petals, many stamens
✿ May–August

Looking like a **white fuzzy ball with its small, feathery flowers**, false bugbane is a bit peculiar even for the decidedly odd buttercup family. It has the cluster of many reproductive parts and the characteristic petal-like sepals typical of buttercups, but after that it becomes eccentric. Having no petals makes it rather unusual (though there are other genera in the buttercup family with this characteristic), but what's really novel is that the showy parts of the bright white flowers are 50–70 tufted stamens! Each of the small flowers in the flat-topped clusters has 3–7 tiny, white sepals that fall off early in summer, leaving only the showy stamens and several pistils.

• The plant may reach 3' in height. The stalked flower clusters project above broad (4–8"), showy, palmately-lobed, toothed leaves.

BUTTERCUP FAMILY

Viola glabella

Tall Yellow Violet

With its cheery, bright yellow flowers and large, shiny, dark green leaves, this early bloomer is a spring delight in Rainier forests. • The tall (to 1') stem bears a few broad, toothed leaves. The showy, long-stalked basal leaves are large (to 4" across), heart-shaped, sharply pointed at the tip, and are usually toothed (sometimes smooth). • Rising above these leaves are the striking flowers—½" **faces of bright yellow with deep purple veins on the lower lip**, especially on the lowest petal, which is broader than the other petals and is somewhat separated from them. As with all violets, the 5 petals funnel into a short nectar spur. • **Related plant:** Round-leaf violet (*V. orbiculata*) grows only 1–2" tall and has a large round leaf (see lower photo).

Typical location: wet clearings in woods and along streams, e.g., creekbank in clearing along trail to Comet Falls (4000'). Also found in subalpine zone. Round-leaf violet can be found along road to Paradise just above bridge over Nisqually River (4000').

Distribution: below 8000'—Cascades and coastal mountains from Alaska to northern California; Sierra Nevada.

Names: *Viola* is Latin for violet. *Glabella* means 'smooth.' Also known as stream violet.

▢ yellow
⬤ 5 petals united in a spur
✿ May–July

Lysichitum americanum

Yellow Skunk Cabbage

Typical location: marshy areas in woods—lower forest zone, e.g., along Trail of Shadows in Longmire area (2700').

Distribution: below 4000'—Cascades and coastal mountains from Alaska to northern California; Rockies in Montana and Idaho.

Names: *Lysichitum* means 'loosening tunic,'—a wonderfully metaphorical reference to the deciduous bract surrounding the cylindrical flower spike. *Americanum*, means 'American.' The common name, skunk cabbage, refers to the plant's large leaves and the flowers' foul odor.

There is nothing subtle about skunk cabbage: its bright yellow (or yellow-green) flowers are massed tightly in a 4–8", **corncob-like spike**; the flower spike is hooded by an even brighter yellow, boat-shaped bract; the **fleshy leaves can be enormous (up to 5' long and 2' wide)**; and the plant stinks (but the smell is apparently delicious to flies!). • Skunk cabbage is an early spring bloomer, filling boggy areas in low to middle elevation forests. After the flowers pass, the leaves continue to grow until they're so large and glossy that they almost don't look real. • In flower or not, skunk cabbage is an impressive and memorable Rainier plant.

■ **yellow**
● **spike of tiny flowers**
✿ **May–June**

ARUM FAMILY

Tolmiea menziesii   **4 PETALS • BLUE/PURPLE**

Youth-on-age

Although all flowers—with their brief phases of buds, blooms, and seeds— remind us of the cycles of life and death, youth-on-age, as the name suggests, provides an especially dramatic example. In autumn, a little plantlet (a short stem with a small, new leaf or 2 at its tip) will grow out of a bud at the base of the mature leaf. When this old leaf withers and falls to the ground, the plantlet is given a chance to root and start the cycle again. • Youth-on-age can grow to 2 ½' tall, its slender flowering stem rising above mostly basal, heart-shaped, toothed leaves. Many of the small (¼") flowers branch off the upper part of the stem. **Four thread-like, brownish-purple petals stick out from between the 5 greenish-yellow sepals**.
• With their splayed, filament-like petals and protruding stamens, the flowers look like they're going to launch off the plant at any moment.

Typical location: streambanks and wet areas in woods, e.g., along Westside Road (2200').

Distribution: below 6000'— Cascades and coastal mountains from Alaska to northern California.

Names: William Tolmie was the Hudson's Bay Company's physician at Fort Vancouver in 1832 and was an avid plant collector in the Pacific Northwest. Archibald Menzies was the naturalist on the Vancouver Expedition in the 1790s. Also known as piggy-back plant. Both common names refer to the 'life from death' plantlets growing from the mature leaves.

■ **brownish purple**
● **4 separate petals**
✿ **June–August**

SAXIFRAGE FAMILY

BLUE/PURPLE • 5 PETALS   *Pinguicula vulgaris*

Butterwort

Typical location: seep areas and bogs in forest clearings, e.g., along upper part of trail to Comet Falls in spray area of falls (4800'). **Uncommon in Rainier.**

Distribution: below 5000'— Cascades and coastal mountains from Alaska to northern California; across northern U.S. and southern Canada.

Names: *Pinguicula* means 'somewhat fat' in reference to the greasy leaf surface. *Vulgaris* means 'common,' though it is not actually common in Rainier. The name butterwort may refer to the greasy leaf or to a belief that the plant improves cows' milk production.

■ violet blue
● 5 petals in a 2-lipped tube
✿ May–August

Small insects that find themselves attracted to the beautiful blue-violet flowers of butterwort, should by all means enjoy the flower but stay clear of the leaves—they're deadly! **'Capturing glands' on the leaf surface make the leaf sticky and slimy**, trapping small insects that are then digested by leaf enzymes—a gruesome death delivered by a plant with such an appealing flower. • The **fleshy, yellowish-green, inward rolled, tongue-like leaves form rosettes** on the ground above which rise the short (to 6") flower stalks, each bearing only 1 of the 1" blue-violet (rarely white) flowers at its tip. The 5 rounded petals unite into a tube that ends in a short spur. • Butterwort usually grows in nitrogen-poor soil and gains additional nutrients by feeding on insects.

Mertensia paniculata   **5 PETALS • BLUE/PURPLE**

Tall Bluebell

Tall bluebell is certainly the perfect name for this flower. When you come across a 'thicket' of these 1–5' plants, heavy with bunches of blue, pendant, bell-shaped flowers, you can almost hear gonging. • The tall stems are thick with 1–6" egg-shaped, blue-green leaves that alternate (usually on short petioles) up the stem. The ½–¾" **flowers occur in loose, limp clusters of a few or many that hang from the ends of the stems**. Each flower is a 5-petaled tube, constricted at the base and a bit more open at the tips. Like the flowers of several other genera in the borage family (e.g., *Hackelia* and *Myosotis*), the flowers of tall bluebell are **pink in bud changing to blue in bloom** (but sometimes you will find a mature flower that is still partly pink).

Typical location: streambanks and seep slopes in forest clearings—upper forest zone, e.g., on seepy slope in clearing along upper part of trail to Comet Falls (4200'). Also found in subalpine zone.

Distribution: below 9000'— Cascades and coastal mountains from Alaska to northern Oregon.

Names: F.C. Mertens (see p. 57). *Paniculata* refers to the flowers occurring in panicles (i.e., branched inflorescences). The common name bluebell describes the color and shape of the flowers.

■ blue (pink in bud)
● 5 petals united in a bell
✿ May–August

BLUE/PURPLE • 5 PETALS　　*Aconitum columbianum*

Monkshood

Though fairly common throughout the mountains of the west, monkshood is infrequent in Rainier. It is an imposing plant with a **stout stem reaching up to 7'** and large (2–8" wide) leaves that are deeply palmately lobed and sharply toothed. But most striking is the 1–2' raceme of **1–2", usually deep blue-purple flowers**. • The flowers (typical of the buttercup family) are quite peculiar. From the side, they look rather like **fat-bodied ducks**; from the front, the 'duck's bill' looks a bit more like a monk's cowl (hood). The most conspicuous parts of the flower (including the hood) are actually the sepals; the 2–5 petals and the thick cluster of many reproductive parts are hidden inside the sepals. • Though usually deep blue-purple, the flowers vary considerably in color all the way to pale blue or even white. • Monkshood is very **poisonous** both to livestock and to humans.

Typical location: streambanks and wet meadows at forest edges—upper forest zone, e.g., around Reflection Lakes (4900'). Also found in subalpine zone.

Distribution: 2000–9000'—Cascades and coastal mountains from Alaska to northern California; Sierra Nevada; Rockies.

■ blue (blue-purple)
● 5 separate petal-like sepals
✿ June–July

Names: *Aconitum* is the ancient Greek name for this plant. *Columbianum* means 'of the west.' The common name, monkshood, refers to the monk's cowl formed by the upper sepal.

BUTTERCUP FAMILY

Viola palustris   **5 PETALS • BLUE/PURPLE**

Marsh Violet

Although several of Rainier's violets are not at all violet (e.g., p. 73), marsh violet is one of those that does remain true to its name. The ¾–1" flowers are **pale blue-violet** with dark purple veins running across the white splotch on the lower middle petal. The **upper 2 petals usually sweep back** demurely. • Each leafless 2–4" stem bears a solitary blossom. The 1–2", heart-shaped leaves are on a separate stem rising from a rhizome or a runner. • Marsh violet is paler and grows in wetter sites than its fellow blue violet *V. adunca* (p. 134). Both are very early spring bloomers.

Typical location: wet openings in woods, marshes, wet meadows, e.g., along Trail of the Shadows at Longmire (2700'). Also found in subalpine zone.

Distribution: 100–5000'— Cascades and coastal mountains in British Columbia and Washington.

Names: *Viola* (see p. 73). *Palustris* means 'of the swamp.'

■ blue (violet)
● 5 petals united in a spur
✿ May–June

Clearings

When you walk in one of the dense woodland areas in Rainier's forest zone, occasionally you will come out into a clearing where trees are largely absent and sun (on a clear day) is abundantly present. Some of these openings—streambanks, boggy fields, seep slopes—are quite wet and host plants that need plenty of water. (See the previous subsection for descriptions of these wet environment forest plants.) However, there are also clearings, sometimes quite large, where the ground is relatively dry (perhaps slightly damp, but not wet). These sunny clearings in the woods—avalanche paths, grassy fields and meadows, road edges—support a variety of fascinating plants different from those you will find in deep forest or on wet soil.

Many families are represented in this open forest environment, but the rose family is especially prevalent here. Some of Rainier's most well-known berry-producing shrubs, as well as some of its most interesting and beautiful flowers, grow here. As you might expect, some of the flowers included in this section can also be found at higher elevations in open subalpine meadows, but they are included here because you will find them most frequently in the forest zone. (Those flowers that sometimes occur in forest clearings, but occur more frequently in the subalpine zone, are included in the subalpine section of this book.)

Along the featured trail and elsewhere: Although the trail to Comet Falls is mostly in the woods, you will find a few places (especially in its upper parts) where it crosses open slopes. Most of the flowers included in this section will be found near the trail on those slopes.

Other easily accessible places to find these forest clearing plants include the Westside Road (part of which you can drive, part of which you have to walk) and meadows and fields in the Longmire area.

Rubus parviflorus | **5 PETALS • WHITE**

Thimbleberry

Thimbleberry is one of the many shrubs in the rose family that populates forest clearings. It is easily recognized by its **large (to 8" long), maple-like leaves and its large (to 2" across), ovate-petaled, white flowers**. This shrub can grow to 10', though 4–6' is more usual. It is non-spiny, which is a real benefit if you ever have to push your way through a dense thimbleberry thicket! • The flower petals are somewhat crinkly. The fruit resembles a bright red raspberry, though some people find it a bit coarse and dry for their taste.

Typical location: clearings in woods and in avalanche paths, e.g., open slope along upper part of the trail to Comet Falls (4500'). Also found in subalpine zone.

Distribution: below 8000'— Cascades and coastal mountains from Alaska to northern California; Sierra Nevada; Rockies; eastern Canada.

Names: *Rubus* (see p. 49). *Parviflorus*, meaning 'small-flowered,' is surely a misnomer, for the thimbleberry flower (up to 2" across) is a giant compared to other *Rubus* species in Rainier, e.g., salmonberry (p. 95), strawberry bramble (*R. pedatus*), and creeping raspberry (p. 49).

▩ **white (fading purple)**
● **5 separate petals**
✿ **June–August**

ROSE FAMILY

Goat's Beard

Despite its large size (up to 6' tall) and its rather rough-looking leaves (large and toothed), goat's beard projects an image of delicacy. The tall stems are surprisingly slender for their height, and the large leaves are divided into several rather graceful, pointed leaflets. • But what gives this plant most of its delicacy is its beard. Many of the **tiny (¼"), white flowers are crowded onto long plumes at the ends of the branches**. Each tiny flower is typical of the rose family, with 5 rounded petals cradling a cluster of thread-like reproductive parts. As the species name indicates, the flowers are unusual in that they are dioecious: some plants have only male flowers, while others have only female flowers.

Typical location: clearings (e.g., roadsides, avalanche tracks, streambanks) in woods, e.g., open slope along upper part of trail to Comet Falls (4500'). Also found in subalpine zone.

Distribution: below 5000'—Cascades and coastal mountains from Alaska to northern California.

Names: *Aruncus* means 'goat's beard' in reference to the long, dangling, fluffy strands of tiny, white flowers. *Dioicus* means 'dioecious'—having separate male and female plants.

■ white
● 5 separate petals
❀ May–July

Sorbus scopulina

Western Mountain Ash

Though identifiable as a rose family member by its 5 separate, regular petals and dense cluster of reproductive parts, the flowers of mountain ash are not the typical rose. Rather, they are small (¼–½"), **creamy white**, and form **densely-packed, round (or flat-topped) clusters**. • Mountain ash is a **large shrub (to 15' tall)** with distinctive compound leaves composed of 9–13 pinnate leaflets. The 1–3" deep green leaflets are narrow, finely toothed, and sharply pointed. • What was delicately attractive in flower becomes strikingly dramatic in fruit—the round berries are glossy, bright red (or orange), and form large clusters.

Typical location: openings in woods and in meadows—upper forest zone, e.g., forest edge along upper part of trail to Comet Falls (4300'). Also found in subalpine zone.

Distribution: 4000–9000'— Cascades and coastal mountains from Alaska to northern California; Sierra Nevada; Rockies.

Names: *Sorbus* is the ancient Latin name for this plant. *Scopulina* means 'of the rocks' in reference to its propensity for growing in rocky openings like avalanche paths. Also known as cascade mountain ash.

■ **white**
● **5 separate petals**
✿ **May–July**

ROSE FAMILY

Campanula scouleri

Scouler's Harebell

Typical location: grassy places and openings in woods, e.g., open slope along upper parts of trail to Comet Falls (4500').

Distribution: 1000–5000'— Cascades and coastal mountains from Alaska to northern California.

Names: *Campanula* means 'little bell' in reference to the shape of the corolla. John Scouler accompanied David Douglas on his botanical excursions through the Pacific Northwest in the early 19th century.

Looking like graceful, twirling ballerinas, or perhaps parachutists searching for a landing spot, the flowers of Scouler's harebell will definitely pique your interest—if you can find them. The plant is only 4–12" tall and tends to bend over, often hiding its flowers among neighboring plants. The ½" flowers have beautiful **white (to pale blue) petals that sweep back in a graceful curve, fully exposing and showcasing the long (½"), straight, pink-tipped style**. The flowers often droop off the usually leaning stems. • The stems are crowded with alternate, toothed leaves.

▪ **white (pale blue)**
● **5 separate petals**
✿ **June–August**

Anaphalis margaritacea **NO/MANY PETALS • WHITE**

Pearly Everlasting

Pearly everlasting has the perfect common name, for whether freshly in bloom or well past its prime and dried out, its **clusters of small, pearl-like, white, dried, crepe-papery flowers** look the same. This appearance is owing primarily to the white, papery, shingle-like bracts that surround the tiny yellowish disk flowers. If you look very closely, you will notice that pearly everlasting is dioecious, i.e., some plants have only male flowers while others have only female flowers. • Each ½–3' stem bears large, flat-topped clusters of the ¼–½" white-wooly flowerheads. Many of the narrow 1–4" leaves alternate up the stem; they are light green or gray above and white-wooly beneath. • Pearly everlasting only has disk flowers; it lacks the showy rays of other composites such as daisies, asters, and arnicas.

Typical location: openings in woods and in meadows, e.g., clearing along upper part of trail to Comet Falls (4500'). Also found in subalpine zone.

Distribution: below 10,000'— Cascades and coastal mountains from Alaska to northern California; Sierra Nevada; Rockies; eastern North America.

Names: *Anaphalis* is the Greek name for everlasting. *Margaritacea* means 'pearl-like.'

■ white
● many disk flowers
✿ July–September

COMPOSITE FAMILY   85

Lilium columbianum

Tiger Lily

Typical location: forest openings and meadows, e.g., open slope along upper part of trail to Comet Falls (4500'). Also found in subalpine zone.

Distribution: below 5500'—Cascades and coastal mountains from British Columbia to northern California; Idaho; Nevada.

Names: *Lilium* is Greek for lily. *Columbianum* (see p. 78).

Tiger lily is a truly spectacular flowering plant for its size, color, and form. As with most members of the *Lilium* genus, tiger lily is a tall (to 4') and robust plant with whorls of narrow, rather leathery leaves and a wide-spreading raceme of many large, nodding flowers. • In tiger lily, the 1–3" **flowers are an intense orange (sometimes more reddish) with red-purple spots. The 6 tepals are strongly recurved,** fully exposing the long, orangish anthers and the pistil, all of which may stick out of the flower an inch or more. When you lie under this plant and look at the orange flowers set against a blue sky, these blossoms look like orange jellyfish floating serenely in an azure sea.

■ orange
● 6 separate petals
✿ June–August

LILY FAMILY

Agoseris aurantiaca

Orange Agoseris

E very time I see this flower, it catches me by surprise. When you think of a dandelion, you probably think yellow, a color this *Agoseris* certainly is not! Perched atop the 4–24" stem is a 1–1½" **solitary, burnt orange sun**—a flowerhead of orange radiating rays with no central 'button' of disk flowers. Like all dandelions, and unlike most composites, orange agoseris has only ray flowers. Although not a common color for wildflowers, orange is not rare; but this burnt-orange color is unique and riveting. As the flowers age, the orange may fade to pink or purple.
• The leaves are basal and narrow, like those of most dandelions, sometimes reaching higher than the plant stem.

Typical location: forest openings and grassy slopes— upper forest zone, e.g., grassy edges of upper part of trail to Comet Falls (4500'). Also found in subalpine zone.

Distribution: 4000–10,000'— Cascades and coastal mountains from Alaska to northern California; Sierra Nevada; Rockies.

Names: *Agoseris* means 'goat chicory.' *Aurantiaca* means 'orange-red.' Also known as orange mountain dandelion.

▪ **orange**
● **many ray flowers**
✿ **June–August**

PINK/RED • 4 PETALS   *Epilobium angustifolium*

Fireweed

Fireweed spreads rapidly and is often one of the first plants to inhabit burned or logged-over areas. I will never forget discovering fireweed in full bloom on the barren ground of mud and ash around Mt. St. Helens just a few months after the eruption (see lower photo).

• Fireweed is not only resilient but also strikingly beautiful; the tall plant stems (up to 6') bear many of the 1–2" flowers along the 1–2' terminal raceme. **The 4 rounded, magenta petals form a delicate cross between which the darker red-purple sepals show through.** In bud, the tightly closed sepals form a rather exotic-looking, deep purple, felty 'torpedo.' As with all species of evening primrose, the ovaries are inferior, (see Names below) swelling voluptuously as the petals begin to fall off. • Fireweed is also striking in autumn, its bronze-scarlet leaves contrasting vividly with its cottony seed tufts.

Typical location: clearings and disturbed areas, e.g., clearings around Reflection Lakes (5000'). Also found in subalpine zone.

Distribution: below 10,000'—Cascades and coastal mountains from Alaska to northern California; Sierra Nevada; Rockies; east to the Atlantic Coast.

Names: *Epilobium* means 'upon the pod' in reference to the inferior ovary (i.e., the petals are attached above the ovary). *Angustifolium* means 'narrow-leaved.'

■ **magenta (red-purple)**
● **4 separate petals**
✿ **June–September**

Corydalis scouleri　　　　**4 PETALS • PINK/RED**

Western Corydalis

Western corydalis is a plant of contrasts and contradictions: it is delicate yet anything but petite; it is highly individual yet often forms dense thickets. • The hollow, rather coarse stem can grow to 4–5' and bears a few large, thin, much-divided leaves. Rising above the leaves is a raceme (or a few racemes) of many (15–35), **oddly shaped, pink (or white) flowers**. Each 1" flower is **tubular with a flaring 'mouth' and a long spur**. Unlike most tubular flowers, the pedicels attach to the middle of the flower tube (not to the end). Because the flowers are arranged horizontally on the stem, they appear to be somewhat precariously perched on their pedicel—a bit like teeter-totters frozen at their balance point.

Typical location: streambanks and openings in woods, e.g., along road from Carbon River to Ipsut Creek (2000').

Distribution: below 5000'—Cascades and coastal mountains from southern British Columbia to Oregon.

Names: *Corydalis* means 'helmet' or 'crested lark' in reference to the odd shape of the flower. John Scouler (see p. 84).

■ **pink (white)**
● **4 petals united in a tube**
✿ **May–July**

POPPY FAMILY (formerly Fumitory Family)

PINK/RED • 5 PETALS | *Stachys cooleyae*

Cooley's Hedge Nettle

Cooley's hedge-nettle is an ideal hummingbird flower with a **long (to 1½") flower tube and a deep red-purple color**. Like most mints, the flowers form 2-lipped tubes and the middle petal of the lower lip is much larger than the other 2 petals. In Cooley's hedge-nettle this lower middle petal forms a broad, projecting scoop.

• The plant can grow to 5' tall though 2–3' is more usual. The **square stem** bears numerous opposite pairs of 1½–4" toothed, egg-shaped leaves on short stalks. Several to many flowers branch off in clusters from the upper foot or so of the stem.• All the petals are a rich red-purple color.

Typical location: openings in woods, e.g., along Westside Road (2200').

Distribution: below 4500'—Cascades and coastal mountains from southern British Columbia to Oregon.

Names: *Stachys* means 'ear of corn' in reference to the long inflorescence. Grace Cooley was a 19th-century American professor.

■ red-purple
● 5 petals in 2-lipped tube
✿ June–August

Castilleja hispida

Harsh Paintbrush

There seems to be at least 1 paintbrush for every Rainier environment. Rocky slopes and cliffs above timberline have the scarlet cliff paintbrush (*C. rupicola*, p. 176), subalpine meadows have the almost florescent magenta paintbrush (*C. parviflora*, p. 131), and low elevation forest openings and meadows have the tall red paintbrush (*C. miniata*) and the smaller (8–16") bright red harsh paintbrush.
• Despite its name, harsh paintbrush gently lights up forest edges and grassy openings with its **delicate but striking red, orange, or even yellow bracts. Its upper bracts are broad and squarish with many (5 or 7) narrow lobes.** The bracts of most paintbrushes are narrow with no more than 3 (sometimes no) lobes. • The leaves and stem are covered with short, stiff, white hairs.

Typical location: forest openings and meadows, e.g., along Westside Road (2200'). Also found in subalpine zone.

Distribution: 1000–5000'— Cascades and coastal mountains from southern British Columbia to Oregon; Montana.

Names: Domingo Castillejo was an 18th-century Spanish botanist. *Hispida* means 'bristly' or 'hairy.'

■ red (orange or yellow)
● 5 petals united in a
   2-lipped tube
✿ May–July

SNAPDRAGON FAMILY

PINK/RED • 5 PETALS | *Nothochelone nemorosa*

Woodland Penstemon

Typical location: woods and rocky slopes, e.g., on edge of clearing along upper part of trail to Comet Falls (4500').

Distribution: from 3000–5000'— Cascades and coastal mountains from southern British Columbia to northern California.

Names: *Nothochelone* means 'false turtle,' perhaps in reference to the vague resemblance of the flower face to a turtle head. *Nemorosa* means 'of the woods.' Also known as woodland beard-tongue. Formerly called *Penstemon nemorosus.*

■ pink-magenta (to red-purple)
● 5 petals united in a 2-lipped tube
✿ June–August

The long (1–1½"),2-lipped tubular flowers possessing 4 stamens and 1 staminode, and the opposite pairs of toothed leaves, may cause you to believe this species belongs to the *Penstemon* genus. However, botanists have put the woodland penstemon into its own genus because of 2 characteristics: 1) the base of each of the filaments of the fertile stamens is densely hairy where it attaches to the corolla, and 2) the filaments are attached to the corolla at the same level. In true penstemons, the filaments of the 4 fertile stamens are attached to the corolla at different levels and their bases are smooth and hairless. • This **tall (to 3') plant bears several (usually 2–5) of the intensely pink-purple (to maroon) flowers along its upper stem**. The anthers are heavily wooly. The **stems usually lean** or grow horizontally.

SNAPDRAGON FAMILY

Digitalis purpurea   **5 PETALS • PINK/RED**

Foxglove

Foxglove is a plant of paradoxes: beautiful yet despised; poisonous yet medicinal. • Stems can reach 6' tall and bear scores of 1½–2½" tubular flowers that range from **white to a rich pink-purple with darker purple spots inside. The flowers droop thickly from one side of the stem**, producing a mass of intense color and intriguing form. Foxglove is an alien introduced from Europe and Africa that spreads rapidly and threatens native plants, so some people dig it up. • People have died from ingesting the highly toxic leaves, which are also the source of Digitalis (an important heart stimulant for many people with heart disease).

Typical location: forest edges, fields, disturbed areas—lower forest zone, e.g., open slope along White River near White River Campground (3500').

Distribution: below 4500'—Cascades and coastal mountains from southern British Columbia to northern California; northern Sierra Nevada; eastern Canada and U.S.

Names: *Digitalis* means 'finger,' perhaps in reference to the long, tubular corolla. This may also be the source of the common name foxglove, or the name may simply be a corruption of a word for 'fox bells.' *Purpurea* means 'purple.'

■ red-purple (pink or white)
● 5 petals united in a 2-lipped tube
✿ June–July

PINK/RED • 5 PETALS   *Aquilegia formosa*

Crimson Columbine

Typical location: openings in woods and in meadows, e.g., open slope along upper part of trail to Comet Falls (4500'). Also found in subalpine zone.

Distribution: below 10,000'— Cascades and coastal mountains from Alaska to northern California; Sierra Nevada.

Names: *Aquilegia* means 'eagle,' probably in reference to the flower's 'talons,' i.e., nectar spurs. *Formosa* means 'beautiful.' The common name, columbine, means 'dove-like,' perhaps in reference to the fancied resemblance of the oddly shaped flowers to a group of sitting doves.

■ red (orange)
● 5 odd-shaped petals
✿ May–August

Crimson columbine is a beautiful and dramatic flower, as much for its yellow as for its crimson. The 5 red sepals flare out to form most of the breadth of these 2" flowers; the 5 **petals are yellow on the tips and extend back into long, red nectar spurs**. Adding to the blaze of yellow is the cluster of long-protruding stamens with conspicuous bright yellow anthers. • Many of the flowers nod on long pedicels that arch off the tall (to 3') plant stem. The flowers rise up to an erect posture once they are pollinated. Being tubular and red, they are pollinated primarily by hummingbirds. • The mostly basal leaves are thin and divided into 3 leaflets that are subdivided into 3 lobes. These delicate leaves are the perfect accompaniment to the graceful, dancing flowers.

Rubus spectabilis   **5 PETALS • PINK/RED**

Salmonberry

Though some species of *Rubus* may have fruits more delicious, none have flowers more beautiful. This 6' shrub, sprinkled with **remarkably deep and bright pink-purple** blooms, will grab and hold your attention. • As a member of the rose family, the 5 separate petals surround a central cluster of reproductive parts. The yellow stamens and dark green leaves make the rich color of the petals seem all the more intense and amazing. This plant entices even after the flowers fade because the fruits that follow are large and raspberry-like (sometimes red, but more often yellowish or orangish). They can be a bit mushy but are delicious, especially on a hot day. • The leaves of salmonberry are compound with several (usually 3) toothed, ovate leaves, typical of many rose family members.

Typical location: damp openings in woods and along streambanks, common on open slope along upper part of trail to Comet Falls (4500').

Distribution: below 5500'— Cascades and coastal mountains from Alaska to northern California.

Names: *Rubus* (see p. 49). *Spectabilis* means 'spectacular' or 'showy.' The common name, salmonberry, is an apt description of the color of some of the berries; some berries are more red in color.

■ **pink-purple (magenta)**
● **5 separate petals**
✿ **May–July**

Self-heal

Typical location: forest clearings, along forest edges, fields, e.g., on open, grassy slope along upper part of trail to Comet Falls (4500').

Distribution: below 8000'—Cascades and coastal mountains from Alaska to northern California; Sierra Nevada; most of U.S.

Names: *Prunella* is derived from a German word for 'quinsy'—a disease that a European species of this genus was thought to cure. *Vulgaris* (see p. 76). The common name, self-heal, refers to the many healing properties of this plant.

■ blue-purple
  (pink-purple)
● 5 petals united in a
  2-lipped tube
✿ June–August

S elf-heal is found on every continent and throughout the U.S. This intriguing plant with intricate flowers rewards a close look. The 4–20" **stem is square** (as are the stems of many members of the mint family) and bears **several pairs of opposite, tongue-like leaves**. The upper pair flares out like wings just below the spike-like cluster of flowers, which looks like a **pinecone with purplish bracts**. • The unopened, velvety buds are a gorgeous blue-purple. The open flowers look like funny, fuzzy faces partly hiding under pink-purple hoods. The upper lip of the tubular flower forms the hood; the lower lip has 3 lobes, the center lobe being larger and fringed. • Self-heal is beautiful and practical, with many medicinal uses.

Rocky Areas

In the forest zone you will occasionally encounter mostly bare, rocky ground so inhospitable that nothing but lichen would seem likely to be able to survive there. This rock environment is indeed difficult for plants. Sheer rock walls, cliffs, shifting talus slopes, or hot and dry, gravelly glacial moraines are certainly not ideal places for most plants to grow. But, if you take the time to carefully explore and examine these rock environments, you will find that they are home to some tenacious plants with exquisite flowers.

As you would expect, the plants of this environment need special adaptations to survive. Look for leaves especially suited to dry conditions—fleshy, leathery, or waxy. Many of these plants will also have deep, flexible roots, but please do not dig them up to look!

Many of the plants that are found in rock crevices or on gravel or boulder slopes in the forest zone also extend into similar environments in the subalpine zone. For plants that grow in the rocks or on gravelly ridges near and above the tree limit, refer to the alpine section.

Along the featured trail and elsewhere: There are a few places where the trail to Comet Falls switchbacks among boulders or crosses talus slopes. Many flowers of the rocky areas of the forest zone can be found in these places. To find some of the other flowers, you could try searching the rock walls along the Steven's Canyon Road or looking along parts of the Westside Road, on the talus slopes and cliffs along the Pinnacle Peak Trail, or among the gravel and boulders along White River—especially up toward the snout of Emmons Glacier out of which the river pours. **Be careful** not to get too close to the glacier, because it is highly unstable and dangerous, hurling rocks every so often at the too-bold explorer.

Lewis monkeyflower at White River

Oxyria digyna

Mountain Sorrel

Despite its barely noticeable flowers, mountain sorrel is a joy to find in the rocks: its tenacity amazes and inspires you, and its leaves put the pizzazz back in your step! • You will usually notice the distinctive **blue-green, kidney-shaped** leaves before the flowers. They are large (2–3") and grow on long stalks from the base of the plant. A nibble on a fresh leaf (not in the national park, of course!) will give you a jolt—depending on your taste, it is deliciously tangy or unpleasantly sour. • Above the leaves rises a slender stem (4–12") bearing a **spike of the tiny, scaly flowers**. They are greenish-white or greenish-yellow (sometimes reddish) in bloom, turning red or reddish-brown in fruit.

Typical location: rock crevices and talus slopes—upper forest zone, e.g., rocks along upper part of trail to Comet Falls (4500'). Also found in subalpine and alpine zones.

Distribution: 4000–13,000'— Cascades and coastal mountains from Alaska to northern California; Sierra Nevada; Rockies; across Canada and northern U.S.

Names: *Oxyria* means 'sour,' in reference to the tart-tasting leaves. *Digyna* is of uncertain meaning, but it may refer to the double styles on the ovary.

■ greenish (reddish in fruit)
● 4 petal-like sepals
✿ July–August

Small-flowered Alumroot

Typical location: rock crevices and talus slopes, e.g., rock wall along Westside Road (2200'). Also found in subalpine zone.

Distribution: below 8000'— Cascades and coastal mountains from southern British Columbia to northern California; Sierra Nevada; Idaho.

Names: Johann von Heucher was an early 18th-century German professor of medicine. *Micrantha* means 'small-flowered.'

- white
- 5 separate petals
- June–August

While some rock plants of the forest zone boldly announce their presence with blazing color, alumroot is almost as conspicuous in its subtlety. Look on rock walls for small cracks and you may see the wispy white flowers of alumroot dancing and sparkling in the sun. • Its leaves are large (to 3") and striking (5–7 lobed and toothed); its flowers are **tiny (¼" or less) and arranged in loose, open clusters**. The bright white flowers contrast vividly with the tall (to 2'), slender, **reddish stems** and with the typically dark rock background. Because the stems are so tall and thin, the slightest breeze will set them (and the flowers) stirring, creating a shimmering white wave. • The narrow, flaring petals and thread-like, protruding stamens give the flowers a wispy, fringed look.

Saxifraga ferruginea — 5 PETALS • WHITE

Rusty Saxifrage

There are many species of *Saxifraga* in Rainier, several of which are found in rocky environments. They all have mostly basal leaves and slender stems with clusters of small, white, 5-petaled flowers. • In rusty saxifrage, the slender stems rise up to 1' above the **cluster of wedge-shaped, toothed leaves**. Many of the ½" white flowers branch loosely off the upper part of the stems. • Stunning to observe from a distance, this plant also reveals a delicate beauty when viewed up close or through a magnifying glass. Unlike some of the other saxifrages, the petals of rusty saxifrage are **distinctly stalked and are usually of 2 types: the upper 3 are a bit broader than the other 2, and they often have 2 orange-yellow spots**. • When the flower begins to go to seed, the swelling ovary becomes red and rather torpedo-shaped as the petals fall off.

Typical location: wet rocks and gravel, e.g., rocky margins of upper part of trail to Comet Falls (4600'). Also found in subalpine zone.

Distribution: below 8000'—Cascades and coastal mountains from Alaska to northern California; Rockies in Montana.

Names: *Saxifraga* (see p. 71). *Ferruginea* and the common name, rusty saxifrage, refer to the rusty color of the sepals.

- ▥ white
- ● 5 separate petals
- ✿ June–August

SAXIFRAGE FAMILY

Lewisia columbiana

Columbia Lewisia

Columbia lewisia brings a vibrant smattering of pink and red to its rock environment. Rising above a **dense basal rosette of narrow, fleshy leaves** are several slender, often reddish, stems that may reach 1' tall. Branching off the upper part of these stems are loose clusters of many ½" flowers. They may remind you a little of peppermint ice cream, because the **petals are usually white (sometimes pink) with pink stripes** and pink splotches at their tip. As a final splash of color, the 5–6 stamens are red. • As with many members of the purslane family, the number of petals varies (in this case, from 6–11); as with almost all purslanes, there are only 2 sepals. • Often growing with sedums (p. 103), Columbia lewisia helps turn its Rainier rock environment into a glorious canvas of color.

Typical location: gravelly slopes and rock outcrops—upper forest zone, e.g., rocky slopes along Pinnacle Peak Trail (5400'). Also found in subalpine zone. **Uncommon in Rainier.**

Distribution: 4500–7000'—Cascades and coastal mountains from Washington to northern California; Idaho.

Names: Meriwether Lewis made extensive collections of plants on the famous Lewis and Clark Expedition of 1804–06 from St. Louis to the Pacific Northwest. *Columbiana* (see p. 78).

▪ **white (with pink veins)**
● **6–11 separate petals**
❀ **June–August**

Sedum oreganum

Oregon Stonecrop

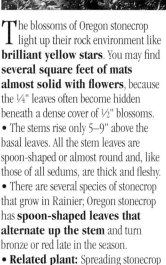

The blossoms of Oregon stonecrop light up their rock environment like **brilliant yellow stars**. You may find **several square feet of mats almost solid with flowers**, because the ¼" leaves often become hidden beneath a dense cover of ½" blossoms.

• The stems rise only 5–9" above the basal leaves. All the stem leaves are spoon-shaped or almost round and, like those of all sedums, are thick and fleshy.

• There are several species of stonecrop that grow in Rainier; Oregon stonecrop has **spoon-shaped leaves that alternate up the stem** and turn bronze or red late in the season.

• **Related plant:** Spreading stonecrop (*S. divergens*) is similar but forms denser mats and has smaller, green or bright red leaves in opposite pairs (see lower photo).

Typical location: gravelly slopes, flats, and rock ledges, e.g., along Westside Road (2200'). Also found in subalpine zone.

Distribution: 3000–6000'— Cascades and coastal mountains from British Columbia to northern California.

Names: There is debate about whether sedum means 'to sit,' or 'to heal.' Many sedums have medicinal qualities. *Oreganum* refers to part of its range.

- ▪ yellow
- ● 5 separate petals
- ✿ July–August

STONECROP FAMILY

Penstemon rupicola

Cliff Penstemon

Typical location: rock ledges and rocky outcrops—upper forest zone, e.g., in rocks along Pinnacle Peak Trail (5400'). Also found in subalpine zone.

Distribution: 4000–7000'— Cascades and coastal mountains from Washington to northern California.

Names: *Penstemon* means '5 stamens' in reference to the sterile (without an anther) 5th stamen. *Rupicola,* meaning 'growing on cliffs and ledges,' says it all about the flower's habitat. Also known as rock penstemon.

■ red (rose-purple)
● 5 petals united in a 2-lipped tube
✿ July–August

Cliff penstemon may be the most dazzling of all Rainier's rock environment flowers below timberline. Its almost **neon pink or scarlet or rose-purple flowers** seem to ignite the rocks. The flowers are enormous in comparison to the leaves and stems, and the **shrubby mat**, not more than 6" tall and dense with roundish ¼" leaves, boasts scores of 1–1 ½" tubular blossoms. • When in bud the flowers are a rich, saturated, shiny scarlet! • There is a narrow elevational band in the subalpine zone where the ranges of cliff penstemon and Davidson's penstemon (a mostly alpine plant of the rocks, see p. 180) overlap. The contrast of the red of the former and the blue of the latter is stunning. Sometimes these 2 close relatives hybridize and produce an intermediate color.

Monardella odoratissima | **5 PETALS • PINK/RED**

Pennyroyal

Coming across a cluster of penny-royal on a barren rocky or sandy flat is a delight for the nose as well as for the eye. The small, opposite, ovate leaves give off an incredibly **pungent aroma** that can envelop you in a mint haze. • The flowers are small (¼") but form **dense, fuzzy heads about 1" wide**. Sometimes they are a creamy white that nearly blends into the environment, but more frequently in Rainier they are a dramatic rose or lavender, standing out vividly from their surroundings. • Stand among a cluster of blooming pennyroyal and let the radiating blossoms and leaves swirl their sweet fragrance around you.

Typical location: dry, rocky slopes—upper forest zone, e.g., dry, glacial moraine along White River (4200'). Also found in subalpine zone.

Distribution: 2000–9500'—Cascades and coastal mountains from Washington to northern California; high desert from eastern Washington to Nevada.

Names: *Monardella* means 'small *Monarda*' (the genus of bee balm, another mint). *Odoratissima* is in reference to the plant's powerful aroma. Also known as western balm.

■ rose or purple (white)
● 5 petals united in a
  2-lipped tube
✿ June–August

Subalpine Zone
(about 5000–7000')

As beautiful and alluring as the lush forests and their flowers are, go a little higher and you will discover the wildflower gardens for which Rainier is world famous. In the strip between the dense forests below and the alpine zone and snowfields above lie intensely velvety-green, rolling subalpine meadows fed by snow-melt and sun.

Velvety-green from a distance, that is, but when observed up close the meadows boast astonishingly vivid palettes of riotous colors: reds, yellows, oranges, whites, blues, and purples. These subalpine parks of Rainier offer some of the most spectacular and celebrated wildflower displays. For variety and profusion, for interest and beauty, for heart-warming color and form these displays are incomparable.

This subalpine section is divided into 2 special environments, each with its own specially adapted plants:

OPEN SLOPES & MEADOWS

WET AREAS

Determine what kind of environment you're in and turn to the appropriate subsection of this book to find your flower.

Subalpine meadow

SUBALPINE ZONE

A few stretches of Rainier's roads reach up into the subalpine zone, most notably the roads ❶ Paradise and ❷ Sunrise. Driving along the last mile or so of the road to Sunrise at 6400'—crossing huge, open, green meadows and facing directly at the mountain—is an awesome experience.

The only easily accessible trails into the subalpine meadows are at ❸ Paradise (see featured trail, p.109) and at ❹ Sunrise (where you can wander on paved paths above the parking lot and out along Sourdough Ridge). Longer, more challenging hikes to wildflower meadows include ❺ Berkeley Park (about 7 miles round-trip from Sunrise), ❻ Grand Park (3 miles beyond Berkeley Park), and ❼ Van Trump Park (a continuation of the Comet Falls Trail featured in the forest zone section).

Map printed from TOPO! © 1997 Wildflower Productions (www.topo.com)

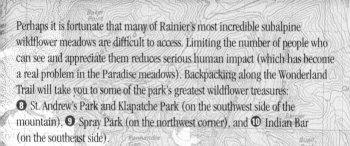

Perhaps it is fortunate that many of Rainier's most incredible subalpine wildflower meadows are difficult to access. Limiting the number of people who can see and appreciate them reduces serious human impact (which has become a real problem in the Paradise meadows). Backpacking along the Wonderland Trail will take you to some of the park's greatest wildflower treasures: ❽ St. Andrew's Park and Klapatche Park (on the southwest side of the mountain), ❾ Spray Park (on the northwest corner), and ❿ Indian Bar (on the southeast side).

Featured Trail

PARADISE

(WANDERING FROM 5400' TO AS HIGH AS 7200')

The wildflower meadows on the slopes above Paradise are justifiably renowned, so you probably won't be alone as you wander the network of mostly paved paths. Start on any of the paths above the giant parking lot and wander to your heart's content. You will begin at about 5400' and can climb as high as 7200' at Pebble Creek. The flowers are profuse—depending on the time of year and what the winter's been like, you may see huge masses of a single

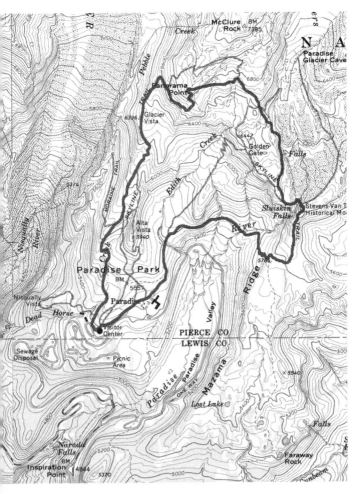

flower (e.g., avalanche lily or subalpine lupine) or large fields with all sorts of colors and species. You will find almost all of the flowers that are described in the subalpine section of this book somewhere in the Paradise meadows.

Lewis monkeyflower at Paradise

And if one of the world's great wildflower displays isn't enough for you, the trails at Paradise can also lead you up the snowfields toward Camp Muir (a staging ground at 10,000' for climbs to the summit) or across them to the Paradise Glacier. (The glacier has melted back and thinned so much that the former ice caves have collapsed.)

Paradise Trail and flower field

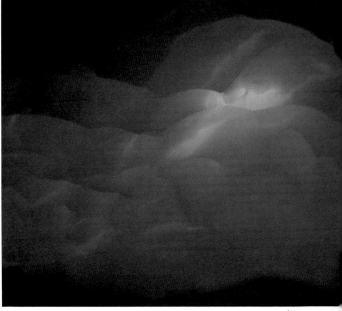

Ice caves

Special environments and flowers along featured trail: You can spend hours wandering on the trails above Paradise without a map or a plan. You will come to many intersections (marked with destination and mileage); just follow your whims. Beautiful flowers and expansive views await any choices you make.

Although all paths here lead into 'paradise,' you might consider the following loop (or variations of it) to encounter an especially wide variety of environments and flowers.

Take the paved trail leading up the slope directly across the parking lot from the Paradise Inn's front door. Bear right (east) at your first choice point and you will be on the Skyline Trail headed toward Sluiskin Falls, the Van Trump Monument, and the Paradise Glacier. The trail will stay more or less level for about ¾ of a mile, crossing gorgeous subalpine parks thick with colorful lupine, paintbrush, cinquefoil, valerian, beargrass, red heather, white heather, bracted lousewort, daisy, aster, bluebell, veronica, spiraea, avalanche lily, glacier lily, arnica, bistort, pasqueflower, corn lily, and mountain ash.

You will cross several rushing creeks lined with monkeyflower, marsh marigold, coltsfoot, and shooting star. And, as if the flowers weren't enough, the glorious white dome of Mt. Rainier provides a stunning backdrop as you look uphill to the gardens.

You will then begin switchbacking up onto Mazama Ridge with panoramic views of the jagged Tatoosh Range to the south. On a hot summer day, the sweet fragrance of the lupine fills your nose and your soul and eases your strenuous climb. The avalanche lily gets thicker as does the yellow bracted lousewort. At 1.4 miles, you will pass the Lakes Trail going down to your right to Reflection Lake, which is a wonderful trail for huckleberries and even the occasional bear. As your trail climbs around a knoll, you will likely encounter some late-lying snow in the hollows but thick, sensuous gardens on the sunny, exposed ridges—coiled lousewort, small-flowered penstemon (both blue and white varieties), phlox, lupine, paintbrush, daisy, veronica, valerian, and pasqueflower. In the shade look for ram's-head pedicularis and showy Jacob's ladder.

At 1.9 miles you will encounter the Stevens-Van Trump Historical Monument and the trail to the Paradise Glacier.

Continuing on the Skyline Trail, you will drop down to cross a small bridge over a gushing creek. Here along the creek you will probably find stunning gardens of pink Lewis monkeyflower, yellow monkeyflower, and yellow willow-herb all growing on a floor of lush, bright green moss.

You will have to brace yourself for a steep climb up the rocky and often snow-covered trail until you intersect with the Golden Gate Trail at 2.5 miles, which returns precipitously across more gorgeous hillside gardens to Paradise (2.4 more miles). However, if you have the energy and the desire to forego descending the Golden Gate Trail, head up the Skyline Trail .9 miles more to magnificent Panorama Point and then on to Pebble Creek. On the way, you will pass the last of the scattered and stunted trees (at about 6500') and you will enter the magical land above the tree limit with its own fascinating flowers (see the alpine section starting on p. 155).

At Pebble Creek, you will see the way up the snowfield ahead to Camp Muir (at 10,000'). This tough but wonderful hike will take you up toward the 'heart' of the mountain, but if you decide to stay in the world of flowers, turn back onto the Skyline Trail loop and switchback your way down to Paradise. You will have several alternative routes back; whichever way you choose, by the time you get back you will have hiked about 5–6 miles and will have climbed about 1800' from Paradise to Pebble Creek. The glories of the mountain will be in your blood and in your lungs, and the magnificent subalpine flowers will be in your heart; you will have seen most of the flowers included in the subalpine zone (and perhaps many of the flowers in the alpine zone as well).

Open Slopes & Meadows

A bove the dense forest and below the alpine fellfields and permanent snow, between the rushing creeks and the occasional clusters of trees, you will find the open meadows and slopes of Rainier's subalpine parks. Usually damp from snowmelt, but not soggy or wet (see the next subsection for the flowers of the wet subalpine areas), these parks are justifiably famous for their wildflower gardens.

Painted on a canvas of rich green grass, you will find vivid floral masterpieces. Sometimes these are a glorious riot of diversity; sometimes they are a magnificent monotony of splendor. Though there are several species you can find in large, nearly homogeneous masses (e.g., subalpine lupine, Cascade aster, mountain arnica, partridge foot), the most frequent and renowned are the lilies—avalanche lilies and glacier lilies. On slopes in the Paradise area and in some of the parks along the Wonderland Trail (e.g., Spray Park), you will find large rolling meadows that are nearly solid with both of these lilies (especially in July).

Along the featured trail and elsewhere: To see the most spectacular wildflower meadows in Paradise, wander along the lower trails from the parking lot (5400') up to about 6000' or so. The trails to the Van Trump Monument and to Alta Vista are particularly worthwhile.

If you want to see spectacular subalpine meadow flower gardens without the crowds, hike the Wonderland Trail to Spray Park, Klapatche Park or Emerald Ridge, or hike from Sunrise down to Berkeley Park and Grand Park.

Paradise flower fields

Erythronium montanum

3/6 PETALS • WHITE

Avalanche Lily

Avalanche lily is appropriately named because you often find huge masses of this large (2–4" across), beautiful, white flower seemingly sweeping away everything in their path as they fill a meadow or slope. • A single flower (or sometimes 2 or 3 flowers) nods delicately from the tip of the 6–14" stem. The 6 pointed tepals sweep back at the tips and become pink-tinged with age. The long, yellow anthers and creamy, branched stigma hang down like tassels. • The 4–8" tongue-like leaves are mostly basal and are rather leathery and shiny green. • Avalanche lily blooms shortly after the snow melts.

Typical location: damp openings and meadows, e.g., along Skyline Trail to Van Trump Monument (5600').

Distribution: 5000–6500'— Cascades and coastal mountains from southern British Columbia to northern Oregon; Montana.

Names: *Erythronium* means 'red,' probably in reference to several pink-red species or perhaps to the tendency of the white-flowered species to become pink-tinged with age. *Montanum* means 'of the mountains.' The common name, avalanche lily, refers to this flower's tendency to occur in huge masses.

■ white
● 6 separate tepals
✿ July–August

Beargrass

Beargrass is an imposing and showy plant, bearing large, dense clusters of hundreds of small (¼–½"), creamy flowers along the upper section of its tall (to 5') stems. Several of these stems usually occur together, creating a startling display, easily visible at quite a distance. • The plant is also recognized by its **thick basal clumps of tough, wiry, sharp-toothed, grass-like leaves** that grow up to 2' long. The plant may take 5 or 6 years before it produces flowers; after it flowers and fruits, the entire plant dies, though the dry leaves may persist for some time.

Typical location: meadows and openings in woods, e.g., along Skyline Trail to Van Trump Monument (5700'). Also found in upper forest zone.

Distribution: below 7500'—Cascades and coastal mountains from southern British Columbia to northern California; northern Sierra Nevada; Rockies.

Names: *Xerophyllum,* meaning 'dry leaf,' and *tenax,* meaning 'tough,' both refer to the persistent fibrous leaves. The common name, beargrass, also refers to the leaves and their appeal to hungry bears (though some botanists think the name refers to the musky smell of the flowers).

■ white
● 6 separate tepals
✿ June–August

Pedicularis racemosa

Sickletop Lousewort

Another of the fascinating 'beaked' louseworts of Rainier, sickletop lousewort is distinguished by the color and shape of its flowers, but more easily by the shape of its leaves. The white (sometimes pinkish or purple) flowers can be confused with the white to creamy yellow flowers of *P. contorta* (p. 167), because both have 'beaks' that curve down and somewhat to the side; but sickletop lousewort is easily identified by its **narrow leaves that are toothed but not deeply divided**. • Many of the leaves alternate up the 1–2' stem; the ½" flowers sit loosely in the leaf axils. The leaves are unusual in that those on the upper part of the stem are larger than those on the lower part.

Typical location: around trees and in meadows, e.g., along Skyline Trail near Van Trump Monument (6000'). Also found in upper forest zone.

Distribution: 3000–8000'— Cascades and coastal mountains from British Columbia to northern California; northern Sierra Nevada; Rockies.

Names: *Pedicularis,* meaning 'lice,' refers to a belief that stock animals eating some members of this genus became susceptible to lice infestation. *Racemosa* (see p.66). Also known as ram's horn pedicularis. The names sickletop and ram's horn refer to the shape of the upper 2 petals.

- ▦ white (pinkish or purple)
- ● 5 petals united in a 2-lipped tube
- ✿ July–August

WHITE • 5 PETALS *Rhododendron albiflorum*

White Rhododendron

Although many members of the heath family (including such shrubs as salal, p. 44, kinnikinnick, p. 47, pink heather, p.128, white heather, p. 168, and yellow heather, p. 170) are ever-greens, white rhododendron (like the various huckleberries, pp. 61, 129) is a deciduous shrub that drops its leaves in the fall. • White rhododendron can reach **as tall as 9'. Both the leaves and the creamy white flowers appear to grow in whorls**. The branches are leafy, usually terminating in a cluster of **shiny green leaves** at their tip with several clusters of the 1–2", bowl-shaped flowers at intervals along their length. In the fall the leaves turn wonderful shades of bronze, orange, and red.

Typical location: around trees and in meadows, e.g., just above Paradise parking lot along Skyline Trail (5400'). Also found in upper forest zone.

Distribution: 3000–7000'—Cascades and coastal mountains from Canada to Oregon; northern Rockies.

Names: *Rhododendron* means 'rose tree.' *Albiflorum* means 'white-flowered.'

■ white
● 5 petals united in bowl
✿ June–August

Valeriana sitchensis

Sitka Valerian

Valerian may not be as showy or as spectacular as many of its subalpine meadow neighbors, but there is a gentle, soothing beauty to its rounded clusters of small (¼"), fuzzy, white or pinkish flowers. The blossoms contribute to the soothing effect with their softly sweet fragrance. • Valerian could be confused with one of the white-flowered umbel family species (with their **Queen Anne's Lace-type flowers**), but close inspection of valerian will show that the flowers are not arranged in a true umbel (i.e., the flower stems do not all originate from the same point on the main stem). An easier way to distinguish valerian from the umbels is by the leaves. Valerian **leaves grow in opposite pairs along the ½–2' plant stem, are toothed, and are pinnately lobed with 1 terminal leaflet**.

Typical location: meadows, e.g., along Skyline Trail to Van Trump Monument (5600').

Distribution: 5000–7000'— Cascades and coastal mountains from Alaska (including Sitka) to northern California; Montana.

Names: *Valeriana* may derive from a Latin word for 'healthy' in reference to the plant's many medicinal properties, or it may be after Valerianus, a Roman ruler who is said to have used a species of this plant as a medication. *Sitchensis* refers to the Alaska town of Sitka.

▦ **white**
● **5 petals united in a bowl**
✿ **July–August**

**WHITE
NO/MANY PETALS**

Anemone occidentalis

Pasqueflower

Typical location: rocky slopes and meadows, e.g., along Skyline Trail to Van Trump Monument (5600'); in great masses on trail to Berkeley Park (5800').

Distribution: 5000–10,000'— Cascades and coastal mountains from southern British Columbia to northern California; Sierra Nevada; Montana.

Names: *Anemone* means 'shaken by the wind' in reference to the feathery styles. *Occidentalis* means 'of the west.' Pasqueflower, meaning 'Easter flower,' refers to the early blooming. Also known as western anemone, tow-head baby, or mouse-on-a-stick.

■ white
● 5-8 separate petal-like sepals
✿ June–July

P asqueflower is an early bloomer of subalpine meadows, **often pushing its densely downy stems through the snow** and exploding into bloom soon after the snow melts. Its 5–8 bright white, petal-like sepals are reminiscent of the snow, but its thick cluster of showy, yellow reproductive parts announces spring in no uncertain terms. • The ½–2' stems are covered with soft, white hairs and bear lacy, much-divided leaves. Each stem is topped with a large (1 ½–3" wide), solitary, bowl-like flower. Frequently the plants cluster. • Pasqueflower dazzles early with its bloom and intrigues later with its fruit. The styles elongate to form a fascinating Dr. Seuss-like, silvery, droopy mophead (see lower photo).

Erigeron peregrinus

Mountain Daisy

Mountain daisy is one of the most common flowers of Rainier subalpine meadows, but is no less beautiful for its abundance. Sometimes you will find large, nearly solid patches of these **white to pink or purple** flowers; other times you will find them lightly scattered among a variety of flowers and colors. Either way, they are a delightful addition to the meadow flora. • Each 4–24" stem will usually have a single 1–2" flowerhead at its tip, though sometimes a stem can bear up to 4 flowerheads. The rays are very narrow and crowded, making room for **up to 100 (though usually more like 30 or 40) rays per head**. The 'button' of disk flowers in the center of the head is yellow. • The narrow 1–8" leaves are occasionally spoon-shaped.

Typical location: openings and meadows, e.g., along Skyline Trail to Van Trump Monument (5600'). Also found in upper forest zone.

Distribution: 4000–11,000'— Cascades and coastal mountains from Alaska to northern California; Sierra Nevada; Rockies.

Names: *Erigeron* means 'early old age' perhaps in reference to the white pappus that parachutes the seeds. *Peregrinus* means 'wanderer' in reference to the ease with which the flowers spread. Also known as subalpine daisy.

■ white (pink or purple)
● many ray and disk
   flowers
✿ July–August

**YELLOW/ORANGE
3/6 PETALS** | *Erythronium grandiflorum*

Glacier Lily

Glacier lily is like a **smaller, yellow version of avalanche lily** (p. 117), but it is still large (to 2" across) and showy. Like avalanche lily, the 6 tepals (golden yellow in glacier lily) sweep back at the tips, exposing the long, yellow (sometimes cream or purple) stamens and the conspicuous, branched stigma. Also like avalanche lily, 1 (or sometimes 2 or 3) of the stunning flowers nods from the tips of the 6–14" stems and the plants typically form great masses, sometimes filling entire meadows. Often the 2 lilies grow together, though their blooming periods are somewhat different. If you happen to be in the right meadow during the short time both lilies are in full bloom, you will be dazzled by one of Rainier's most spectacular floral displays. • The 4–8" tongue-like leaves are mostly basal and shiny green.

Typical location: meadows and slopes, e.g., along Skyline Trail to Van Trump Monument (6000').

Distribution: 5000–7000'—Cascades and coastal mountains from southern British Columbia to northern California; Rockies.

Names: *Erythronium* (see p. 117). *Grandiflorum* (see p. 69).

■ **yellow**
● **6 separate tepals**
✿ **June–July**

LILY FAMILY

Pedicularis bracteosa

Bracted Lousewort

Of the several strange louseworts you can find in Rainier, bracted lousewort is the tallest (to 2–3') and the only one with truly **yellow flowers** (there are a couple species with creamy white-yellow flowers). • Many of the large (½–1") yellow (sometimes reddish) flowers crowd in the long (to 7") flower spike atop the stem. With their **hooded beaks** (the upper 2 petals) projecting out beyond the rest of the flower tube (the other 3 petals) and curving down, the flower spike seems to be teeming with inquisitive little cartoon characters straining to get a good look out at the world. • The leaves are typical of louseworts—pinnately compound in narrow leaflets that are lobed or toothed.

Typical location: openings in woods and in meadows, e.g., along Skyline Trail to Van Trump Monument (5600'). Also found in upper forest zone.

Distribution: 4000–7500'—Cascades and coastal mountains from southern British Columbia to northern California; Rockies.

Names: *Pedicularis* (see p. 119). *Bracteosa* means 'bracted' in reference to the modified leaves (bracts) right under the flower spike. Also known as wood betony, which derives from a word meaning 'medicinal plant.'

- yellow (whitish or reddish)
- 5 petals united in a 2-lipped tube
- July–August

**YELLOW/ORANGE
5 PETALS**

Potentilla flabellifolia

Fan-leaf Cinquefoil

Typical location: grassy meadows and rocky places, e.g., along Skyline Trail to Van Trump Monument (5600'). Also found in alpine zone.

Distribution: 5000–12,000'— Cascades and coastal mountains from southern British Columbia to northern California; Sierra Nevada; Montana.

Names: *Potentilla* means 'potent' in reference to the plant's medicinal qualities. *Flabellifolia* means 'fan-leaf' in reference to the fan-like spreading of the 3 leaflets. Also known as Rainier cinquefoil. Cinquefoil means '5 leaves.' Many cinquefoils, though not *P. flabellifolia*, have compound leaves with 5 leaflets.

■ yellow
● 5 separate petals
❀ July–August

Along with arnica (opposite page), cinquefoil is the most common source of **bright yellow or orange** in Rainier's grassy subalpine meadows. As with all members of the rose family, cinquefoil has 5 regular petals and a central clump of many reproductive parts. The petals are somewhat heart-shaped and overlap slightly. • You might confuse cinquefoil with buttercup, but cinquefoil (unlike buttercup) always has 5 **green sepals under the petals with 5 little bractlets between the sepals**.

• Fan-leaf cinquefoil has 3 deeply toothed leaflets spread out in a fan.

• The 1" flowers stay rather close to the ground on 3–12" stems. Early in the season the leaves are pressed against the ground; by the time the flowers bloom, the leaves have lifted a few inches.

Arnica latifolia

Broadleaf Arnica

Whether you find broadleaf arnica in the full sun of a subalpine meadow or a forest clearing or in the partial shade of the woods, its **bright yellow sunflower-like flower-heads** light up their environment and lift your spirits. • Broadleaf arnica may grow to 2' tall; its stem bears **2-4 pairs of opposite, nearly triangular, toothed leaves**. Sometimes this plant has only 1 flowerhead at the tip of its single stem; other times it has 2 or 3 (rarely more) flowerheads with 1 on the tip of the main stem and the others atop secondary stems coming out of the axils of the upper pair of leaves.

Typical location: open slopes and meadows, e.g., open hillsides along Skyline Trail to Van Trump Monument (5500'). Also found in upper forest zone.

Distribution: 4000–7000'— Cascades and coastal mountains from Alaska to northern California; Sierra Nevada; Rockies.

Names: *Arnica* is the ancient Greek name for this plant. *Latifolia* means 'broad-leaf.' Also known as mountain arnica.

- yellow
- many ray and disk flowers
- July–August

PINK/RED • 5 PETALS | *Phyllodoce empetriformis*

Pink Mountain Heather

Typical location: open slopes and meadows, e.g., open hillsides along Skyline Trail to Van Trump Monument (5600'). Also found in alpine zone.

Distribution: 5000–8500'—Cascades and coastal mountains from Alaska to northern California; Rockies.

Names: *Phyllodoce* is the name of a sea nymph from Greek mythology. *Empetriformis* means '*Empetrum*-leafed.' *Empetrum* is the genus name for crowberry, which is another member of the heath family with evergreen, needle-like leaves.

■ **pink (rose-purple)**
● **5 petals united in an urn**
✿ **June–August**

Ranging from a delicate pink to an almost shocking rose-purple the little bells of pink mountain heather light up Rainier hillsides. The plant is an **evergreen shrub** that rarely exceeds 2' in height but often greatly surpasses that in width. The ½" flowers are sometimes so densely crowded on their stems that the shrub becomes a solid blaze of color. • The **dazzling pink-rose of the flowers** is enhanced by **tiny, scarlet sepals** and dark green, needle-like leaves. The flower bells dangle or face upwards.
• As the plant goes to seed, the flower falls off intact, leaving only the swelling ovary, with its long pistil, on the stem.

HEATH FAMILY

Vaccinium deliciosum | **5 PETALS • PINK/RED**

Cascade Huckleberry

Vaccinium deliciosum is indeed delicious: its **pastel pink flowers** are as appealing to the eye as its **succulent, blue berries** are to the tongue. Just remember when you are browsing the berries: bears share your love for this delectable fruit! • All huckleberry species in Rainier are shrubs, but Cascade huckleberry is unusual in that it forms **low mats** rarely exceeding 1' tall. The ¼" pink, bell-shaped flowers are a beautiful contrast to the ½–2" ovate, somewhat pale-green leaves. In fall, Cascade huckleberry makes itself known with the ripening of the juicy berries, followed by the turning of the leaves. When you see almost an entire hillside or meadow burnished with its wine-red fall foliage, you will realize how prevalent this huckleberry is!

Typical location: forest openings and meadows, e.g., along Skyline Trail near Van Trump Monument (6000'). Also found in upper forest zone.

Distribution: 2000–7000'— Cascades and coastal mountains from British Columbia to northern California; northern Sierra Nevada.

Names: *Vaccinium* (see p. 61). *Deliciosum* is self-explanatory! Also known as delicious blueberry.

■ pink
● 5 petals united in a bell
❀ June–August

PINK/RED • 5 PETALS　　*Spiraea densiflora*

Rosy Spirea

Typical location: openings and meadows, e.g., along Skyline Trail to Van Trump Monument (5600'). Also found in upper forest zone.

Distribution: 2000–10,000'— Cascades and coastal mountains from British Columbia to northern California; Sierra Nevada; Rockies.

Names: *Spiraea* means 'wreath' or 'shrub.' *Densiflora* means 'densely flowered.' Also known as subalpine spirea.

S oft in fragrance as well as in appearance, rosy spirea fills the air with a **sweet rose-like aroma**. This small shrub (to about 3' tall) is thick with 1–2" egg-shaped leaves and very dense, **flat-topped or gently rounded clusters of tiny (⅛–¼"), pink to rose flowers**. Adding to its softness are the thick clumps of pink reproductive parts (mostly stamens) sticking up out of the flowers and often obscuring the petals underneath. Unlike some shrubby members of the rose family, spirea is unarmed (i.e., without prickles).

• Spirea's 'rosiness' is not limited to the petals, stamens, and fragrance, because even the bark is red tinged.

■ pink
● 5 separate petals
✿ July–August

Castilleja parviflora
var. oreopola

5 PETALS • PINK/RED

Magenta Paintbrush

The **vibrant pink-purple-magenta** of magenta paintbrush seems to glow as if the flower were generating its own light. You could almost believe that these magenta 'beacons' could light up their subalpine meadows even on the darkest night.

• Like all paint-brushes, the conspicuous color comes not from the petals but from the bracts. The lower leaves on the plant's 6–12" stems are still green and, as in many paintbrushes, are usually 3–5 lobed.

• The **true flowers have atrophied into pale yellowish-green tubes that are mostly hidden by the bracts**. Botanists distinguish several varieties of *C. parviflora* by the color of these bracts, which can range from red to orange and even to white.

Typical location: meadows and slopes, e.g., along Skyline Trail to Van Trump Monument (5500'). Also found in alpine zone.

Distribution: 5000–9000'— Cascades and coastal mountains from Alaska to Oregon; Rockies. Some botanists extend its range to the Sierra Nevada while others call the Sierra species *C. peirsonii*.

Names: *Castilleja* (see p. 91). *Parviflora* (see p. 61).

■ magenta
● 5 petals united in a 2-lipped tube
✿ July–August

**PINK/RED
NO/MANY PETALS**

Cirsium edule

Edible Thistle

With all the gorgeous flowers and stunning flower displays in Rainier's subalpine meadows, you might overlook edible thistle despite its size (**it can reach 6'**), dismissing it as a weed. That would be a shame, for it is a very interesting plant with quite beautiful flowers. • Many thistles (including several in Rainier) are aliens introduced from Europe, but edible thistle is a native, found only in Washington and southern British Columbia. Like all thistles, what appears to be the flower is actually a flowerhead composed of hundreds of thread-like disk flowers. The beautiful **pink-purple flowers** of edible thistle comprise a 2–3" flowerhead supported by a white, cottony involucre (i.e., the set of bracts under the flowers). The flowerhead, especially early in the season, nods from its stem. The leaves are typical of thistles—large (to 1' long), toothed, and spiny.

Typical location: forest openings and meadows, e.g., along Skyline Trail near intersection with Golden Gate Trail (6400'). Also found in upper forest zone.

Distribution: 3000–7000'—Cascades and coastal mountains from southern British Columbia to southern Washington.

Names: *Cirsium* is the ancient Greek name for this plant. *Edule* means 'edible' in reference to the young stalks of the plant that Native Americans (and early explorers Lewis and Clark) found tasty. Also known as Indian thistle.

■ **pink-purple**
● **dense head of spiny disc flowers**
✿ **June–August**

COMPOSITE FAMILY

Lupinus latifolius
var. *subalpinus*

5 PETALS • BLUE/PURPLE

Subalpine Lupine

A subalpine meadow filled with subalpine lupine is like a beautiful blue inland sea. Each **1–3' bushy plant** has several stems ending in long, spike-like racemes of flowers. At peak bloom, each plant can be covered densely with the ½" **blue or blue-purple flowers**. The banner (the upper, vertical petal) usually has a white (or yellow) central patch that turns rosy purple with age. • As with all lupines, the leaves of subalpine lupine are palmately compound, but the leaflets are a bit broader than in most species. • As you walk through a large patch of these striking plants, take a deep whiff of their wonderfully sweet fragrance. • The fruits are hairy pea pods (to 4"), but should not be eaten, because most lupines are at least mildly **poisonous**.

Typical location: forest openings and moist meadows, e.g., along Skyline Trail to Van Trump Monument (5600'), masses in Grand Park (6700').

Distribution: 4000–8000'—Cascades and coastal mountains from British Columbia to northern California.

Names: *Lupinus* means 'wolf,' presumably from the mistaken belief that lupine 'wolf up' nutrients from the soil (actually they are nitrogen-fixing and so can grow in and improve poor soil). *Latifolius* (see p.127). Also known as broadleaf lupine. This species is sometimes considered a subspecies of *L. arcticus*.

■ **blue**
● **5 irregular petals**
✿ **July–August**

BLUE/PURPLE • 5 PETALS — *Viola adunca*

Early Blue Violet

Typical location: forest openings and meadows, e.g., open meadow along Skyline Trail to Van Trump Monument (5600'). Also found in forest zone.

Distribution: below 10,000'— Cascades and coastal mountains from Alaska to northern California; Sierra Nevada; Rockies; eastern U.S.

Names: *Viola* (see p. 73). *Adunca* means 'hooked' in reference to the conspicuous nectar spur. Also known as western long-spurred violet or western dog violet.

Early blue violet adds a delightful splash of rich blue or violet to meadows just emerging from the snow. The plant is short (3–4", elongating to up to 1' in late-season), but the flowers are relatively large (¾" across) and tend to form large clusters. A wild bouquet of these blossoms on their bed of large, round or heart-shaped leaves is a joy to discover. • The **rich violet petals are white at their base and have darker purple veins** (nectar guides to direct bees to the nectar in the spur). The nectar spur, projecting back behind the flower face, is unusually long for a violet, reaching about half the length of the lower petal blade.

■ blue (blue-purple)
● 5 separate petals and nectar spur
✿ May–August

Penstemon procerus | **5 PETALS • BLUE/PURPLE**

Small-flowered Penstemon

There is something cute about the 2-lipped, open-faced, tubular flowers of penstemon (and monkey-flower, pp. 146, 149). The 2 petals in the upper lip flare up, and the 3 lower petals bend down creating a friendly-looking open mouth. • Small-flowered penstemon grows to 2', moderately tall for a penstemon, and bears several pairs of opposite leaves up the stem above a tuft of basal leaves. The ½" long flowers **occur in 2 or 3 distinctively separated, dense clusters that whorl dramatically around the stem**. • The petals are a deep blue-purple with a whitish throat and often a pink tinge (especially on the tube). Occasionally you will find yellowish or whitish flowers (see lower photo).

Typical location: meadows and rocky areas (shorter variety occurs in alpine zone), e.g., both blue and white varieties along Skyline Trail near Van Trump Monument (6000').

Distribution: 5500–10,000'— Cascades and coastal mountains from Alaska to northern California; eastern Washington; central Sierra Nevada; Rockies.

Names: *Penstemon* (see p. 104). *Procerus* means 'tall.' Also known as tall penstemon.

- ■ blue-purple (white)
- ● 5 petals united in a 2-lipped tube
- ✿ June–August

BLUE/PURPLE • 5 PETALS | *Campanula rotundifolia*

Common Harebell

Typical location: openings, meadows, and rocky places, e.g., along Skyline Trail to Van Trump Monument (5600'). Also found in forest zone, e.g., along Westside Road (2800').

Distribution: below 8000'— Cascades and coastal mountains from Alaska to northern California; Rockies; eastern U.S.; across Canada and northern U.S.

Names: *Campanula* (see p. 84). *Rotundifolia* means 'round-leaved.' Also known as bluebells of Scotland.

■ blue
● 5 petals united in a tube
✿ July–August

When you see the large (to almost 1"), beautiful, blue bells of this plant gracing one of Rainier's grassy subalpine meadows, you may start to hear bagpipes and lilting highland accents. These are the bluebells of Scotland celebrated in the poems of Robert Burns. • One (or sometimes several) of the **broad, bell-shaped flowers** nods (sometimes stands erect) from the tip of its slender 2–3' stem. The tips of the 5 petals flare out, opening the tube even wider. The inside of the tube may be paler blue (or even white). The **sepals are very narrow and finger-like.** • The species name *rotundifolia* refers to the round basal leaves that usually wither before the flowers bloom. The leaves you are likely to see are long and grass-like.

HAREBELL FAMILY

*Polemonium
pulcherrimum*

Showy Jacob's Ladder

Look in the shade around trees at the edges of subalpine meadows and you may find some **gorgeous blue eyes** looking back at you. If they have **yellow centers** and are perched atop long (8–15"), **pinnately compound leaves**, they probably belong to showy Jacob's ladder, one of the most elegantly resplendent of Rainier's wildflowers.
• With their 10–15 pairs of small (1"), opposite or offset leaflets, the leaves really do look like ladders. They may be a little too small to climb, but the plant may just take you up to heaven anyway with the beauty of its exquisite blue to lavender, bell-shaped flowers. • The smell of the leaves, however, may bring you back to earth with a thud! They are somewhat reminiscent of a certain black-and-white striped mammal that can clear out a meadow in a hurry!

Typical location: shady areas at edges of meadows, e.g., along Skyline Trail near Van Trump Monument (6000'). Also found in alpine zone.

Distribution: 5000–10,000'— Cascades and coastal mountains from Alaska to California; Sierra Nevada; Rockies.

Names: *Polemonium* is of uncertain origin, possibly named after the Greek philosopher Polemon or perhaps derived from a word for 'strife.' *Pulcherrium* means 'showy.'

■ **blue (violet)**
● **5 petals united in a bowl**
✿ **July–August**

**BLUE/PURPLE
NO/MANY PETALS**

Aster ledophyllus

Cascade Aster

Typical location: open meadows, rocky slopes, e.g., along Skyline Trail to Van Trump Monument (5500'). Also found in upper forest zone.

Distribution: 4000-6500'— Cascades and coastal mountains from Washington to northern California.

Names: *Aster* means 'star' in reference to the flaring rays. *Ledophyllus* means '*Ledum*-like leaves' in reference to the resemblance of the broad, oblong leaves to those of *Ledum* (Labrador tea in the heath family).

■ **purple**
● **many ray and disk
   flowers**
✿ **July–August**

If you look out onto almost any of Rainier's subalpine meadows in July or August when they are in peak summer bloom, you are almost certain to see asters or daisies as part of the wildflower display. Their cheery flowers, with yellow disks and purple or lavender or white rays, seem to complete the meadow scene, bringing a certain stability and balance to the wild assemblage of colors and shapes. • In Cascade aster the **stems (to 3') are thick with broad, pointed leaves** and bear several 1–2" wide, showy flowerheads. Each flower head consists of a **few (6-20) widely separated, lavender purple rays** radiating out from the central 'button' of yellow disk flowers.

Wet Areas

Though open, grassy meadows and slopes comprise much of the subalpine zone in Rainier, there are other more specialized environments, such as under scattered clumps of trees, on rock cliffs and talus slopes, and in very wet areas along creeks and near ponds and lakes.

Most of the plants that thrive under trees in the subalpine zone are either found more frequently in the forest zone or also inhabit the open subalpine meadows. Most of the plants that can be found in subalpine rock environments can also be found in rocky places in the forest zone or in rocky environments above or near the tree limit.

There are, however, many plants that live primarily in very wet environments in the subalpine zone. The following section describes the plants of subalpine streambanks, seeps, boggy flats, edges of ponds and lakes, and soggy hollows saturated with snowmelt.

The flowers and gardens of these wet subalpine areas can rival those of even the lushest of Rainier's famous subalpine meadows. The 'jungles' of monkeyflowers (pink and yellow) are especially spectacular.

Along the featured trail and elsewhere: The trails at Paradise take you to many wet places. There are some especially soggy creekbanks and hollows along the Skyline Trail to Sluiskin Falls and on past the Van Trump Monument. The Lewis monkeyflowers are spectacular where the trail drops down from the monument to cross a run-off.

One of the great wet environment gardens in Rainier stretches along the stream in Berkeley Park where masses of monkeyflower intermingle with lupine, valerian, daisy, arnica, hellebore, laurel, coltsfoot, shooting star, and many others in unrestrained exuberance. Less spectacular but easier to access are the wet gardens around Reflection Lake. If you backpack, you will find wonderfully lush and diverse gardens along the creek at Indian Bar.

Monkeyflowers at Indian Bar

Veratrum viride

3/6 PETALS • WHITE

Green False Hellebore

Green false hellebore is an alluring, dramatic, and **poisonous** plant. It can grow **up to 6' tall and has large (6–12"), strongly-veined, cabbage-like leaves**. Do not make the fatal mistake of confusing this plant with skunk cabbage (p. 74), which is edible. Although skunk cabbage and hellebore look completely different when they're in bloom, their leaves do look somewhat similar when the plants first come up. • Hellebore may be dangerous, but it is certainly dazzling. Sometimes you will find a jungle of these plants filling a soggy meadow, their long racemes of **greenish flowers** reaching high above almost every other plant. Look closely at the flowers—their dark green centers deepen their mystique.

Typical location: streambanks and wet meadows, e.g., near creek along Skyline Trail to Van Trump Monument (5500').

Distribution: 5000–7000'—Cascades and coastal mountains from Alaska to northern California; Rockies; eastern North America.

Names: *Veratrum* means 'dark roots.' *Viride* means 'green' in reference to the unusual yellowish-green color of the flowers. Also known as corn lily, which refers to the plant's corn-like leaves.

▨ **greenish**
● **6 separate tepals**
✿ **June–August**

Polygonum bistortoides

Bistort

Typical location: streambanks and wet meadows, e.g., near creek along Skyline Trail to Van Trump Monument (5600').

Distribution: 5000–10,000'— Cascades and coastal mountains from Alaska to northern California; Sierra Nevada; Rockies; eastern North America.

Names: *Polygonum* means 'many knees' in reference to the swollen nodes on the stems of some species. *Bistortoides* means 'twice twisted' in reference to the way the individual flowers are arranged on the raceme.

■ white (pale pink)
● 5 tiny petal-like sepals
❀ July–August

Despite its rather **suspect aroma** (which reminds some people of sweaty socks) and its tiny, unspectacular flowers, there's something about bistort that many find appealing. • The nearly bare 1–2' stems (the leaves are mostly basal) lift their modest **thumbs of tiny white flowers** up among (or above) their showier neighbors with bold self-confidence (in the above photo, the bistorts are the small, cylindrical flowerheads among the larger mopheads of pasqueflowers in seed). The fluffy, papery sepals and the fuzzy stamens give bistort a soft, gentle appearance. The flowerhead is intricately beautiful in bud, with tinges of red at the base of the tightly braided sepals.
• The basal leaves are long and narrow; there are a few much smaller stem leaves.

Heracleum lanatum | **5 PETALS • WHITE**

Cow Parsnip

Cow parsnip is one of the few herbaceous plants that can rival hellebore (p. 141) for size and robustness. You sometimes find these 2 giants growing together in seeps or wet meadows, and cow parsnip will usually be the taller plant. • The **thick, hollow stem can grow to 8' or even 10' and bears very large leaves (up to 1' long and 1' wide)** with 3 toothed lobes and almost as large (4–10" across) umbrella-like flowerheads. These heads are composed of numerous clusters of tiny (⅛–¼") flowers, each at the tip of an umbrella-like spoke. The resulting **double umbel form, with its radiating symmetry,** is typical of the umbel (or carrot) family, and is, in my 'umbel' opinion, an exquisite piece of botanical design.

Typical location: along streams and in wet meadows, e.g., along stream on Skyline Trail to Van Trump Monument (5600'). Also found in forest zone.

Distribution: below 8000'— Cascades and coastal mountains from Alaska to northern California; Sierra Nevada; Rockies; eastern and southern U.S.

Names: *Heracleum* is derived from Hercules in reference to the plant's enormous size. *Lanatum* means 'wooly' in reference to the dense, white hairs on the stem.

■ white
● 5 tiny petals united in saucer
✿ July–August

Caltha leptosepala
var. *biflora*

Marsh Marigold

Typical location: wet, marshy places (including icy snow runoff), e.g., creek edges along Skyline Trail to Van Trump Monument (5500'). Also found in alpine zone.

Distribution: 3000–11,000'— Cascades and coastal mountains from Alaska to northern California; Sierra Nevada; Rockies.

Names: *Caltha* means 'bowl-shaped' in reference to the flower. *Leptosepala* means 'slender-sepaled' in reference to the 5–11, narrow, petal-like sepals. *Biflora* means '2-flowered' in reference to there usually being 2 (sometimes 1) flowers per stem. Formerly called *C. howellii*.

- ■ white
- ● 5-11 petal-like sepals
- ✿ June–July

Marsh marigold is an early bloomer in wet subalpine meadows (typically along with buttercup) often when there is still snow close by and ice-cold water trickling and pooling underfoot. If you explore one of these meadows at night in early summer, you may well find marsh marigold in full bloom above a sheet of ice! • The flowers are large (to 1½" across) and **stunningly white** in contrast to their lush, waxy green, **round or kidney-shaped leaves**, which can be up to 4" long and broad. The **5–11 petal-like sepals** surround a clump of bright yellow reproductive parts. • There is debate over whether or not the 2 similar forms of marsh marigold should be separated into 2 species (*C. leptosepala* and *C. biflora*). One type has broad leaves while the other has long leaves.

Petasites frigidus
var. *nivalis*

Sweet Coltsfoot

Sweet coltsfoot seems to love the wettest, coldest areas. You will often find it in oozy seeps where ice-cold water saturates the ground. It's probably noticed less for its flowers than for its stems and basal leaves: the ½–1½' stems are thick and ribbed; the leaves are very broad (up to 16") and deeply palmately lobed and/or toothed. Both the stems and the undersides of the leaves are usually finely hairy or even densely wooly. • The flowers are not showy, but they are intriguing. The narrow, flat-topped flowerheads are crammed with whitish (or pink or purplish) ray flowers and pink to purple disk flowers. You may notice that not all flowerheads look alike; this is because some flowerheads have primarily female flowers while others have mostly male flowers, and the 2 types of flowerheads have different proportions of ray and disk flowers. • **Related plant:** Tall coltsfoot (*P. frigidus* var. *palmatus*) grows to 3' tall in wet openings of low elevation forests. It blooms early in masses along low elevation roads.

Typical location: seeps, streambanks, and soggy meadows, e.g., mossy seep along Skyline Trail to Van Trump Monument (5500').

Distribution: *P. frigidus* var. *nivalis* ranges from 4000–7000' in the Cascades and coastal mountains from Alaska to Washington.

Names: *Petasites* means 'broad-brimmed hat,' referring to the broad leaves. *Frigidus* means 'of cold regions.' *Nivalis* means 'of the snow.' Also known as butterbur.

- white (pinkish or purplish)
- many ray and disk flowers
- June–August

Mimulus tilingii

Mountain Monkeyflower

Typical location: seeps and streambanks, e.g., along Skyline Trail with *M. lewisii* near bridge below Van Trump Monument (5800'); at Indian Bar (5100'). Also found in alpine zone.

Distribution: 5000–11,000'— Cascades and coastal mountains from Alaska to northern California; Sierra Nevada; Rockies.

Names: *Mimulus* means 'little mime' or 'mimic' in reference to the flower faces. Heinrich Tiling was a Baltic physician and botanist who collected in California and Nevada for various European botanical gardens.

- yellow
- 5 petals united in a 2-lipped tube
- July–August

Although mountain monkeyflower is **yellow** and Lewis monkeyflower (p. 149) is red-purple, they both frequent wet streambanks (and sometimes streambeds), have large, showy flowers, and tend to grow in spectacular masses. As if to emphasize their parallels, these dazzling monkeyflowers often grow together in glorious counterpoint. • Mountain monkeyflower is a much smaller plant than Lewis monkeyflower, **rarely exceeding 1' tall and often growing much shorter (3" or so)**. The 1" flowers almost seem too big for the plant. You will find large patches of wet ground carpeted by the blossoms, completely hiding the stems and opposite pairs of ovate leaves.

Epilobium glaberrimum

4 PETALS • PINK/RED

Smoothstem Willow-herb

You can find the small, delicate flowers of smoothstem willow-herb along creeks or in damp, grassy meadows in the subalpine zone, usually partly hidden among their larger neighbors. • Although the flowers are small, the slender stems can grow up to 3' tall and are thick with opposite pairs of deep green, ovate leaves. The stems appear to terminate in long (1–2"), smooth, somewhat swollen segments, on top of which are perched the **delicate ½", 4-petaled flowers**. After the petals shrivel and these 'stem segments' swell to become much thicker, it becomes obvious that they are actually inferior (i.e., under the petals) ovaries. This is diagnostic of the evening-primrose family. • The pink or white petals are notched about ⅓ of their length.

Typical location: along creeks, damp meadows, e.g., along Skyline Trail to Van Trump Monument (5500'). Also found in forest zone.

Distribution: 2000–10,000'— Cascades and coastal mountains from Alaska to northern California; Sierra Nevada; Rockies.

Names: *Epilobium* means 'upon pod' in reference to the inferior ovary above which the petals are attached. *Glaberrimum* means 'smooth' in reference to the hairless stem.

■ **pink (white with pink streaks)**
● **4 separate petals**
✿ **July–August**

PINK/RED • 5 PETALS *Dodecatheon jeffreyi*

Jeffrey's Shooting Star

Typical location: streambanks and wet meadows, e.g., along creek up Skyline Trail to Van Trump Monument (5600').

Distribution: 3000–10,000'— Cascades and coastal mountains from Alaska to northern California; Sierra Nevada; Montana.

Names: *Dodecatheon* means '12 gods,' perhaps indicating that the flower is protected by the Greek pantheon of gods. John Jeffrey was a 19th-century gardener at the Edinburgh Botanical Gardens.

■ pink
● 4 or 5 petals united
at base
✿ June–July

It's always a joy to come across shooting star. In early summer **clusters of the magenta flowers hang nose-down from their arching pedicels** atop the ½–2' plant stem. • The petals bend back like an umbrella in the wind and point upward, as if to trace their fall from the sky. The black-maroon 'nose' enfolding the reproductive parts is left exposed. The pink petals have a white or yellow band at their base. • When you feel in a quiet, observant mood, sit beside a shooting star and watch a bee hang upside-down on the 'nose,' pulling the flower and pedicel down with its weight like a bungee jumper at the end of the tether. • The 1–8" leaves are basal and narrowly elliptical with smooth edges. A few or many (3–18) of the ½–1" flowers branch off the top of each stem.

Mimulus lewisii   **5 PETALS • PINK/RED**

Lewis Monkeyflower

Lewis monkeyflower may be the quintessential flower of Rainier's wet environments and may even rival avalanche lily (p. 117) for Rainier's signature flower. It is large and richly colored, produces occasional albinos for interest and contrast, and often grows in magnificent, showy masses. It is also named after one of the great explorers of the Pacific Northwest. • Each 1–3' plant bears numerous pairs of 1–3" distinctively veined, toothed leaves. Coming out of the leaf axils are long (to 3") pedicels, each supporting 1 of the 1½–2" flowers. The 5 petals flare out of a 2-lipped tube into a face. The entire flower is an **exquisite, deep rose-purple; the lower 3 petals have ridges marked with yellow and speckled with silvery hairs**.

• Even in bud, Lewis monkeyflower is gorgeous, with deep purple, ridged sepals opening slightly to show the intensely rose 'baby' petals wound tightly inside.

Typical location: seeps and streambanks, e.g., along Skyline Trail near bridge below Van Trump Monument (5800'), at Indian Bar (5100').

Distribution: 4000–9500'—Cascades and coastal mountains from British Columbia to northern California; Sierra Nevada (paler pink flowers); Rockies.

Names: *Mimulus* (see p.146). *Lewisii* is after Meriwether Lewis (see p. 102). Also known as pink monkeyflower.

■ red-purple
● 5 petals united in a 2-lipped tube
❀ July–August

Pedicularis groenlandica

Elephantheads

Typical location: streambanks and very wet meadows, e.g., along stream in Berkeley Park (5800'). Also found in alpine zone.

Distribution: 3000–12,000'— Cascades and coastal mountains from Alaska to northern California; Sierra Nevada; Rockies; eastern North America.

Names: *Pedicularis* (see p. 119). *Groenlandica* means 'of Greenland,' though elephantheads doesn't actually occur there!

- ◾ pink (red-purple)
- ● 5 petals united in a 2-lipped tube
- ❁ July–August

Birds' beaks, ram heads, sickles, and now elephant heads! Of all the bizarre creatures in the genus *Pedicularis* (pp. 119, 125, 177), elephantheads may be the strangest. The upper part of the ½–2' stem is crowded with **stacks of ½" pink elephant heads with ears alert and trunks uplifted**. • The 2 petals of the flower tube's upper lip are united like a beak that resembles an elephant trunk, out of which projects the tiny stigma. If you lift the trunk, the bright yellow anthers that were tucked under it will pop out. Bees shake pollen onto their bodies while struggling to get at the nectar. • The plant has typical fern-like *Pedicularis* leaves, which are pinnately divided and toothed and basal. • The plants often grow in extensive clusters.

Kalmia microphylla   **5 PETALS • PINK/RED**

Bog Laurel

Bog laurel is a perky flower with a clever pollination tactic. Early in the blooming, you will find the 10 black anthers neatly and tightly pressed into little pockets on the petals, creating the impression that the petals are black-spotted. As the season progresses, the filaments lengthen but the anther's remain 'pocketed,' so the filaments bend, creating 'spring-loaded' anthers. When triggered by an insect visitor, the filaments spring up and the anthers 'salt' the insect with pollen. • The **½–¾" saucer-shaped flowers** are clustered on long stalks at the tips of the highest branches. • The plant is a **low, evergreen shrub** (although sometimes as high as 2') whose 1" elliptical, leathery leaves are dark green on the top side and gray-green beneath.

Typical location: soggy soil, especially around ponds, lakes, and streams, e.g., along creek in Berkeley Park (5800').

Distribution: 5500–10,000'— Cascades and coastal mountains from Alaska to northern California; Sierra Nevada; Rockies.

Names: P. Kalm, a student of Linnaeus (see p. 62), traveled in North America in the 18th century. *Microphylla* means 'small-leafed.' The name bog laurel comes from the similarity of *Kalmia* leaves to those of true laurel (*Umbellularia* in the laurel family). Also known as alpine laurel. Also called *K. polifolia* var. *microphylla*.

■ pink (rose purple)
● 5 petals united in a saucer
✿ July–August

HEATH FAMILY

BLUE/PURPLE • 4 PETALS   *Veronica cusickii*

Cusick's Veronica

Typical location: streambanks and wet meadows (and sometimes rocky slopes), e.g., along Skyline Trail to Van Trump Monument (5500').

Distribution: below 9000'—Cascades and coastal mountains from southern British Columbia to northern California; Sierra Nevada.

Names: *Veronica* is possibly named after Saint Veronica. William Cusick was an Oregon plant collector of the early 1900s. Also known as Cusick's speedwell. Speedwell probably refers to the plant's purported medicinal qualities.

■ violet (blue-purple)
● 4 petals united in a
  2-lipped tube
❀ July–August

Of all the blues, blue-purples, and violets at Rainier, the color of Cusick's veronica may surpass them all for richness and sensuality. It is a small plant (only 4–8" tall) with small, ¼–½" flowers. Each flower has **4 petals** (the upper large one is actually 2 petals fused together) of a **deep, saturated violet with darker purple veins** and a white splotch at the base. Protruding from the shallow bowl-shaped flowers are 2 long, delicate stamens and an even longer, slender pistil. • The stems are leafy with 1" ovate, opposite leaves. The upper stem has a raceme of flowers, intensifying the color with sheer numbers.

Gentiana calycosa · **5 PETALS • BLUE/PURPLE**

Mountain Bog Gentian

Rainier lavishes most of its subalpine gifts on mid-summer: lush green hills, rushing water, blue-sky days, and meadows thick with flowers. However, visitors who linger are rewarded with a few of Rainier's special treasures. In late August and even early September, weeks after the peak blooming in subalpine meadows, bog gentian achieves its full bloom. As the leaves turn and moods deepen, this gentian is a last voice for the playful days of summer. • The **1–1½" blue trumpets** reach straight up from the tips of their low (4–10") stems, sounding their call for all to hear. The 5 petals are purple-streaked and flare out at the tips. The **fringes between the petal tips** add a note of grace. • Opposite pairs of small, fleshy leaves are attached directly to the plant stem.

Typical location: streambanks and wet meadows, e.g., along Paradise Trail to Alta Vista (6000'), large clusters near Summerland on Wonderland Trail (6000').

Distribution: 4000–13,000'— Cascades and coastal mountains from British Columbia to northern California; Sierra Nevada; Rockies.

Names: *Gentius*, is named after a king of ancient Illyria, who is said to have discovered the plant's medicinal value. *Calycosa* means 'cup-like' in reference to the shape of the calyx.

■ blue
● 5 petals united in a tube
✿ August–September

Alpine Zone

(above 7000')

Although in many places in Rainier the lush subalpine meadows are bordered by permanent snow and ice or by inhospitable, precipitous rock, there are a few accessible rocky ridges and gravelly flats above these meadows (and above the tree limit, which ranges from about 6500–7000' in Rainier) where flowers can still thrive.

Reaching this rugged alpine environment above the trees, where winds howl unabated and cold is always on the prowl, reveals an amazing world of extremes and contrasts. It is a place of vast vistas and endless skies and the ever-present white mountain; yet it is also a place of delicate gardens of miniature plants, where the smallest detail is intimately linked with survival. A small rock becomes a fortress for a dwarfed plant hiding from the wind; a small hollow, still damp from just-melted snow, becomes a watering hole for tiny, thirsty plants. Cushion plants, with mounds or even spheres of tiny leaves packed tight against the world outside, may manage only a fraction of an inch of leaf growth each year.

Approaching Frozen Lake from 1st Burroughs Mt.

As you would probably expect, no roads exist to take you into this alpine world; you will have to hike. The hike will be steep and there are only a few trails. You may find some alpine plants ❶ around and above Panorama Point in the Paradise area and ❷ on the ridges above Panhandle Gap on the Wonderland Trail. But by far the best (and most accessible) place in the park to see alpine plants is ❸ along the trail from Sunrise (or from White River and Glacier Basin) to the Burroughs Mtns. (1st, 2nd, and 3rd, see featured trail, p. 158).

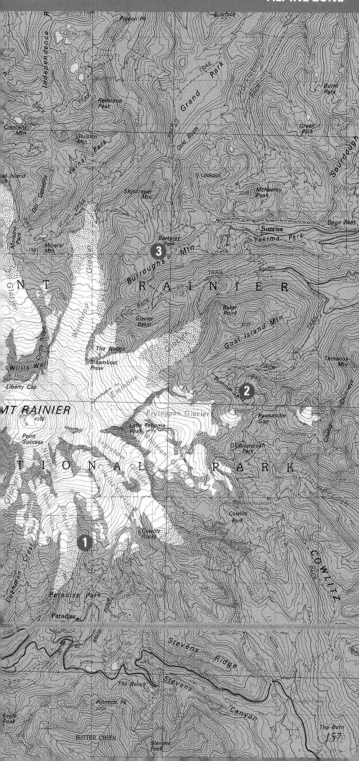

Featured Trail
BURROUGHS MOUNTAIN

(3.5 MILES TO 2ND BURROUGHS MT., 1000' CLIMB FROM SUNRISE TO ABOUT 7400'; 1.0 MILE AND 600' MORE CLIMB TO 3RD BURROUGHS MT.)

From the Sunrise parking lot you will walk up the paved path to the ridge, and then west past the intensely blue Frozen Lake. A short distance later you will begin the climb on a rocky trail (sometimes partly buried by snow) into the austere and hauntingly beautiful alpine world. You will climb and climb and climb until you swear the next step is the summit of Mt. Rainier itself—which actually is still almost 7000' above you!

You will see mats and cushions and hairy stems and dwarf blossoms and all sorts of floral wonders—a unique community of plants that you will probably appreciate all the more for the effort and commitment it took for you to get there!

As a bonus reward, you will be able to look down on the green meadows of Glacier Basin where there's a good chance you will see a herd of elk. You will also be very likely to see mountain goats between 2nd Burroughs and 3rd Burroughs mountains, and from the top of 3rd Burroughs you

View from 2nd Burroughs Mt.

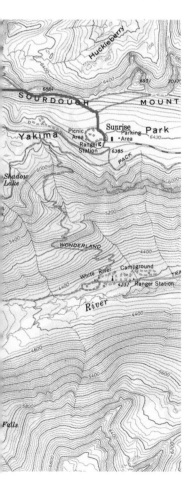

will be looking straight down into the azure-tinged crevasses of Winthrop Glacier. Except for the climb to Mt. Rainier's summit, this trail is probably the most stunning and ethereal hike in the park.

Although most of the plants of the alpine zone live only in that zone, you will occasionally find some alpine species on rocky and exposed areas below the tree limit as well.

Special environments and flowers along featured trail: As you climb from Sunrise toward the alpine zone, the trees will get scarcer and more stunted. Shortly after Frozen Lake, you will encounter a sign announcing your entry into the alpine tundra, after which you will see no trees—except for an occasional solitary struggler trying to hide from the wind behind a rock, looking more like a wind-carved shrub than a tree. For the most part, you will be crossing wide-open tundra where rocks, flowers, and animals are the only 'bumps' on the landscape. If you're lucky, you will see marmots, mountain goats, and elk; if you're observant, you will probably see at least 30 species of alpine flowers.

From the sign (at about 6800'), the trail steeply ascends to 1st Burroughs Mt. (about 1 mile with 300' of climbing). Along the way, you will see rocky slopes covered with wild-flowers, all hugging the ground to stay out of the wind. Some flowers form dense, nearly impenetrable cushions, while most form loose, squat clusters gently contouring the ground.

Look for clusters of partridge foot, alpine lupine, cliff paintbrush, coiled-beak lousewort, Jacob's ladder, the 3 heathers (red, yellow, and white), Davidson's penstemon, golden daisy, pussytoes, knotweed, northern goldenrod, arctic sandwort, smelowskia, alpine buckwheat, pussypaws, catchfly, and agoseris. You will also find many tight clusters of phlox, an occasional rounded shrub of bush cinquefoil, and 1 or 2 gorgeous cushions of moss campion.

You will need excellent balance and plenty of nerve on parts of this climb to 1st Burroughs Mt. because in most years you will have to cross a few steep snowfields covering the trail. **Be careful**. You will eventually reach the flat top of 1st Burroughs Mt. and a trail intersection (2.2 miles back to Sunrise the way you came or 2.7 miles via Sunrise Lake). The alpine lupine, alpine aster, and coiled-beak lousewort are especially spectacular on this flat.

Then 2nd Burroughs Mt. awaits you; it will only be another 300' climb and about a mile to this windswept plateau. On the way you will encounter many now-familiar flower friends. The clumps of yellow heather practically cover the hillside in places. After a brief rest on the stone chair atop 2nd Burroughs Mt., you may decide to climb that last knoll up ahead. The trail will descend a bit before climbing another 600' or so. You may see mountain goats in the saddle before you meet the trail to Glacier Basin careening down over the side.

After passing several more fields of wildflowers, you will be standing atop 3rd Burroughs Mt. (about 8000') and looking down a cliff onto Winthrop Glacier. In a good flower year, you might be amazed at how many flowers are blooming at the very top: you are likely to see patches of lupine, golden daisy, partridge foot, Tolmie's saxifrage, yellow heather, alpine buckwheat, Davidson's penstemon, and knotweed just for starters. From the top of 3rd Burroughs Mt., it will look like the summit of Mt. Rainier is just an easy stroll away—remember though, looks can be deceiving!

Smelowskia calycina

Smelowskia

Because this is a mustard with the name smelowskia, you might think that this plant would be quite fragrant, but it's not—the name has nothing to do with being smelly (see Names right). *Smelowskia* is an appealing plant with a soft, delicate appearance that adds a touch of subtle color to its often gray, **rocky, alpine habitat**. • The deeply cut gray-hairy leaves are mostly basal. The 2–10" stems rising above the mat of leaves bear numerous flowers in clusters. The small (¼"), **4-petaled flowers are a soft off-white color**. The sepals fall off shortly after the flowers bloom.

Typical location: rocky flats and ridges, e.g., rocks around Frozen Lake (6800').

Distribution: 6000–10,000'— Cascades from Alaska to Washington; Nevada; northern Rockies.

Names: Timotheus Smelowski was a 19th-century Russian botanist. *Calycina* means 'without a calyx' in reference to the sepals falling off soon after the flowers bloom.

■ **white**
● **4 separate petals**
✿ **July–August**

WHITE • 5 PETALS

Saxifraga tolmiei

Tolmie's Saxifrage

Typical location: rocky slopes and talus fields, e.g., along trail up 1st Burroughs Mt. (6900').

Distribution: above 6000'—Cascades and coastal mountains from Alaska to northern California; Sierra Nevada (uncommon); Idaho; Montana.

Names: *Saxifraga* (see p. 71). William Tolmie (see p. 75). Also known as alpine saxifrage.

■ white
● 5 separate petals
✿ July–August

Like many of its alpine neighbors, Tolmie's saxifrage forms low, dense mats of tiny (⅛–⅜") leaves. The **leaves are shiny, green, and smooth**, not densely hairy or gray-green like the leaves of most alpine plants. Tolmie's saxifrage has adopted an alternative strategy to prevent desiccation and tissue damage from radiation—the leaves are shiny to reflect sunlight and are thick and fleshy to retain moisture. Also, the plant usually grows where snow lies late into summer, so the ground stays somewhat damp for most of the growing season.

• Each ½" bloom has **5 widely separated, ovate petals flaring out into a star**; between the petals are what look like smaller petals but are actually the 5 stamens. After pollination when the ovary begins swelling, its **2-beaked ovary** turns reddish, loudly announcing its fertility!

Elmera racemosa

Elmera

Elmera is like a mitrewort (p. 70) or a fringecup (p. 69) of the rocks. Like its 2 close relatives of the saxifrage family, elmera has **petals that are rather oddly fringed** or lobed, giving them an airy, wispy appearance.
• Elmera's **leaves are mostly basal and kidney-shaped** with the scalloped edges typical of many saxifrages. Each 4–12" stem bears many (10–35) ¼" yellowish-white flowers in a spike. • A close look at the flowers will reveal amazingly delicate and intricate petals, which are lobed into 3–7 tiny, feathery 'mittens.' Deep inside the flower cup are 5 bright yellow, orange, or white anthers. It seems that only saxifrages can combine such profound strangeness with such enticing delicacy!

Typical location: rock crevices and talus slopes, e.g., in rocks along trail to Frozen Lake (6700'). Also found in subalpine zone.

Distribution: 5000–8000'— Cascades and coastal mountains of Washington and Oregon.

Names: *Elmera* honors Adolph Elmer, a collector of Washington State plants. *Racemosa* (see p. 66).

▩ white
● 5 petals united in a cup
✿ July–August

SAXIFRAGE FAMILY

WHITE • 5 PETALS   *Minuartia obtusiloba*

Arctic Sandwort

Typical location: rocky ridges and flats, e.g., along trail up 1st Burroughs Mt. (7000'). Also found in upper subalpine zone.

Distribution: 6500–11,000'— Cascades and coastal mountains from Alaska to northern California; Sierra Nevada; Rockies.

Names: J. Minuart was an 18th-century Spanish botanist and pharmacist. *Obtusiloba* means 'blunt lobes' in reference to the rounded petals. Formerly called *Arenaria obtusiloba*.

▪ **white**
● **5 separate petals**
✿ **July–August**

Arctic sandwort is another of the mat-forming alpine plants, though its mat tends to be looser than most. You will usually find open spots in the mat where you can see the rocky ground beneath. Adding to this loose appearance are leafless 2–3" flower stems that lift the flowers noticeably above the glandular leaves. The plant stems spread horizontally and root at intervals, giving the mat multiple anchors and considerable tenacity. • The ½–¾" flowers are subtle and exquisite **satiny white stars**. The 5 petals have round tips and short greenish veins at the base. The light green ovary and the pale **pink anthers sticking out of the flower** help give it a delicate, pastel tone. Each stem bears only 1 flower at its tip.

Luetkea pectinata

Partridge Foot

Though the flowers of partridge foot are tiny (¼") and the stems are short (only to 6"), the plant is very showy. Partridge foot is a **prostrate, evergreen, sub-shrub that can form large mats** (up to several yards in diameter) that are thick with creamy white flowers. • Each tiny flower is a typical rose family member with 5 separate petals and a cluster of many reproductive parts (about 20 stamens and 4–6 pistils). Each stem bears a narrow raceme thick with flowers. Partridge foot creates quite a display— a large mat of plants, each stem with scores of flowers, and each flower with dense clusters of reproductive parts. • The **small leaves are much-divided into tiny, linear segments** (presumably resembling the toes on a partridge's foot).

Typical location: meadows and rocky areas, e.g., in rocks along trail to 3rd Burroughs Mt. (7800'). Also found in subalpine zone.

Distribution: 6000–9000'— Cascades and coastal mountains from Alaska to northern California.

Names: Count F.P. Luetke was a 19th-century Russian explorer and sea captain. *Pectinata* means 'like the teeth of a comb' in reference to the cleft leaves. The common name partridge foot also refers to these leaves.

■ white (cream)
● 5 separate petals
✿ July–August

WHITE • 5 PETALS   *Polygonum newberryi*

Newberry's Knotweed

Typical location: rocky slopes and flats, e.g., common along trail up 3rd Burroughs Mt. (7800'). Also found in subalpine zone.

Distribution: 5000–8000'— Cascades and coastal mountains from Washington to California; Sierra Nevada.

Names: *Polygonum* (see p. 142). John Newberry was a 19th-century surgeon and naturalist.

- ▦ white (to pink)
- ● 5 petal-like sepals
- ✿ July–August

Though alpine gardens are often surprisingly profuse with colorful and showy flowers, you will sometimes encounter a rocky slope or flat above timberline that appears to be flowerless. But often, even in these seemingly barren places, if you look closely, you may find more in bloom that you suspected.

• Newberry's knotweed initially appears to be a leafy, prostrate, flowerless plant, but **partially hidden among the broad leaves are clusters of tiny, greenish-white (sometimes pink), crepe-papery flowers.** They aren't particularly showy, but can nonetheless form subtle and delicate gardens all by themselves, growing in masses on bare, rocky slopes. In the fall, these knotweed gardens are set ablaze as the clusters of **leaves turn bright scarlet** (see lower photo).

166   BUCKWHEAT FAMILY

Pedicularis contorta

Coiled-beak Lousewort

Although not that unusual for a *Pedicularis*, coiled-beak lousewort is still a rather odd-looking flower. As with all members of the genus, the upper 2 petals unite to form a **beak, which in this case curves down from the top somewhat like the letter 'S.'** Several of the ½" creamy white (to pale yellow) flowers branch off the 4–16" stem in a loose spike. • The leaves are basal and fern-like, deeply dissected into opposite, finger-like segments. Small, green bracts with narrow lobes occur under the flowers all the way up the stem.

Typical location: meadows and around trees, rocky flats, and slopes, e.g., great masses along trail between 2nd and 3rd Burroughs Mtns. (7000'). Also found in subalpine zone.

Distribution: 5000–8000'— Cascades and coastal mountains from southern British Columbia to northern California; Rockies.

Names: *Pedicularis* (see p. 119). *Contorta* means 'twisted' in reference to the flower's down-curving beak.

▨ white (cream)
⬤ 5 petals united in a 2-lipped tube
✿ July–August

SNAPDRAGON FAMILY

WHITE • 5 PETALS   *Cassiope mertensiana*

White Mountain Heather

Typical location: snow-melt slopes and rocky ridges, e.g., rocky slope along trail up 1st Burroughs Mt. (7000'). Also found in subalpine zone, e.g., moist slopes along Paradise Trail to Sluiskin Falls (5600').

Distribution: 5500–11,000'— Cascades and coastal mountains from Alaska to northern California; Sierra Nevada; Montana.

Names: *Cassiope* was the mother of Andromeda in Greek mythology. Franz Mertens (see p. 157). Also known as moss heather, which refers to the resemblance of its tightly leaved, scaly-looking branches to the branches of clubmoss.

▇ white
● 5 petals united in an urn
✿ July–August

White mountain heather is a low, evergreen shrub that brings a special gift to its alpine and subalpine homes. In full bloom, a shrub may be almost completely covered by **hundreds of small (¼"), white bells** dangling in bunches from short, slender stalks at the tips of the branches. It may take only a soft breath of wind to tremble these bells, and you could swear you hear music. • Because the flowers are nodding, the sepals are on top in full view. These just might be the most attractive non-petal-like sepals of any Rainier flower. They are 5 slender, scarlet fingers delicately and gracefully holding the bells in place. • The stems of this shrub spread out horizontally and rarely exceed 1½' in height. The tiny (⅛–¼"), scale-like, ovate leaves overlap to create a braid-like effect.

Antennaria alpina
var. *media*

Alpine Pussytoes

Although alpine pussytoes is an inconspicuous plant, a close look at the flowers reveals some interesting details and a subtle beauty. • The **small, spoon-shaped, basal leaves are densely white-wooly and form compact mats**. The 1–6" stems and their few, narrow leaves are also densely hairy. Several (2–9) tight flowerheads cluster at the tip of each stem. • The bushy flowerhead is composed entirely of **pearly white** (sometimes yellowish) disk flowers, which project above brownish-green or black, sharply pointed bracts. Careful examination reveals that some plants have only male flowers, while others have only female flowers. • Gently rub the flowerheads (or leaves or stems), and you may be reminded of a soft, furry kitten.

Typical location: rocky slopes and flats, e.g., along trail up 1st Burroughs Mt. (7000'). Also found in upper subalpine zone.

Distribution: 6000–12,000'— Cascades and coastal mountains from southern British Columbia to northern California; Sierra Nevada; Rockies; across Canada and northern U.S.

Names: *Antennaria* means 'antenna' in reference to the thread-like, protruding pappus. *Alpina* means 'alpine.' *Media* means 'intermediate' in form between 2 species. The common name pussytoes refers to the clusters of small, furry flowers. Also known as *A. media*.

◼ **white**
⬤ **many disk flowers**
✿ **July–August**

Phyllodoce glanduliflora

Yellow Mountain Heather

Typical location: moist slopes, rocky ridges, e.g., along trail up 3rd Burroughs Mt. (8000'). Also found in upper subalpine zone.

Distribution: below 9000'— Cascades and coastal mountains from Alaska to Oregon; Wyoming.

Names: *Phyllodoce* (see p. 128). *Glanduliflora* means 'gland-bearing flower' in reference to the glandular hairs covering the petals, sepals, and flower stalks.

■ yellow (greenish white)
● 5 petals united in an urn
✿ July–August

Yellow mountain heather frequently grows with the very similar white mountain heather (p. 168). Both are low, evergreen shrubs with tiny leaves and small flowers nodding in clusters off slender stalks at the tips of the branches. In full bloom, both can become almost completely covered with flowers. • The leaves of yellow mountain heather are needle-like, the flowers are **yellowish or greenish-white urns puckered in a kiss,** and the sepals are more or less the same color as the petals. • The flowers are tacky-sticky from the glandular hairs. • Of the 3 Rainier heathers, yellow mountain heather will be found at the highest elevations. In the subalpine zone it often hybridizes with pink mountain heather (p. 128). Some people call the pale pink hybrid *P. intermedia.*

YELLOW/ORANGE
5 PETALS

Potentilla fruticosa

Shrubby Cinquefoil

Shrubby cinquefoil is a stunning plant. Its bright yellow flowers, typical of the many cinquefoil species, seem even brighter and more exuberant growing on a **dense shrub**. Some plants are less shrubby (more like regular herbs with only a few stems and flowers), but most are shrubs, a few inches to 2–3' tall, and thick with leaves that hide the rocky ground underneath. Shrubby cinquefoil creates its own landscape of soft, rolling hills of gray-green leaves. • Scattered on this undulating, leafy landscape are scores of **1" showy flowers**. As with all cinquefoils, the 5 broad petals surround a thick central cluster of yellow reproductive parts. • The bark is typically reddish brown and (especially on younger stems) it shreds in long strips.

Typical location: moist areas on rocky slopes, e.g., along trail to 2nd Burroughs Mt. (7300'). Also found in subalpine zone.

Distribution: 6000–12,000'— Cascades from Alaska to northern California; Sierra Nevada; Rockies; eastern North America.

Names: *Potentilla* (see p. 126). *Fruticosa* means 'shrubby.'

■ yellow
● 5 separate petals
✿ July–August

ROSE FAMILY

171

**YELLOW/ORANGE
NO/MANY PETALS**

Erigeron aureus

Alpine Golden Daisy

Typical location: rocky ridges and flats, e.g., along trail up 2nd Burroughs Mt. (7200'). Also found in upper subalpine zone.

Distribution: 6000–8000'— Cascades and coastal mountains from southern British Columbia to Washington.

Names: *Erigeron* (see p. 123). *Aureus* means 'golden.'

Alpine golden daisy is as bright and cheery as its name suggests. Clusters of the large (¾–1"), yellow flowerheads light up their rocky, wind-swept homes above timberline. As with many alpine flowers, the solitary flower-heads look enormous poised atop their dwarfed (1–6") stems. • Other alpine adaptations for golden daisy include the small (1"), basal leaves and the hair-iness of the leaves, stems, and bracts under the flowerheads. • Each flower-head is quite a burst of yellow—**a central 'button' of scores and scores of orange-yellow disk flowers surrounded by an incredible number (as many as 70!) of yellow ray flowers**. In this harsh environment with a short growing season, the large number of flowers on each flowerhead increases the odds for this plant to get pollinated and set seed.

- yellow
- many ray and disk flowers
- July–August

Agoseris glauca

Short-beaked Agoseris

You may think that a dandelion is just a dandelion, but Rainier boasts a few dandelions that are exceptionally striking and beautiful. The flowerheads of short-beaked agoseris (unlike those of orange agoseris, p. 87) are the expected bright yellow color but are unexpectedly large (1¹/₂–2" wide). The flowerheads appear even larger on the dwarfed plants found on higher alpine ridges. Short-beaked agoseris can grow 2' at lower elevations, but 6–10" is more usual in the alpine zone. • As with all dandelions, the flowerheads consist of ray flowers only. • The long (to 12"), narrow leaves are basal.

Typical location: rocky slopes and flats, e.g. along trail up 2nd Burroughs Mt. (7300'). Also found in subalpine zone.

Distribution: 5000–12,000'— Cascades and coastal mountains from British Columbia to northern California; Sierra Nevada; Rockies.

Names: *Agoseris* is the old Greek name for chicory. *Glauca* means 'glaucous,' i.e., covered with a whitish, powdery film in reference to the leaves.

- ■ yellow
- ● many ray flowers
- ✿ July–August

COMPOSITE FAMILY

173

YELLOW/ORANGE
NO/MANY PETALS

Solidago multiradiata

Northern Goldenrod

Although you can find northern goldenrod throughout the zones of Rainier and can sometimes find it growing in masses in grassy meadows, it is most dramatic when you discover it blooming in splendid solitude among the rocks above timberline. • Its 1–4", **tongue-like, basal leaves** are striking and unusual for alpine plants, for they are smooth and bright green instead of hairy and gray-green. Rising above these basal leaves are 2–12" stems bearing **tight clusters of small (¼–½") bright yellow flowerheads**. Each head consists of 10 or so ray flowers surrounding 10–30 disk flowers. There may be only a few heads per cluster or there may be many; either way the clusters bring exuberant color to their environment.

Typical location: rocky flats and slopes, grassy meadows, e.g., along trail up 2nd Burroughs Mt. (7300'). Also found in upper forest and subalpine zones.

Distribution: 3000–11,000'— Cascades and coastal mountains from Alaska to northern California; Sierra Nevada; Rockies.

Names: *Solidago* means 'make well' in reference to purported medicinal value of the plants. *Multiradiata* refers to the many flowerheads in the inflorescence.

■ yellow
● many ray and disk flowers
✿ July–August

COMPOSITE FAMILY

Calyptridium umbellatum

Pussypaws

The alpine zone presents difficult conditions to plants, not the least of which is the often harsh, dessicating wind. • The **spoon-shaped leaves** of pussypaws are excellent examples of how the leaves of alpine plants growing above tree line are specially adapted to minimize the evaporating effects of the wind. They are **tiny and fleshy and are pressed tightly to the ground**. The **bright green** leaves are easily distinguishable from those of other alpine plants because they are not covered by hairs and they grow in a tight, low, symmetrical **rosette** where each leaf minimizes exposure to the wind but maximizes exposure to the sun. • Radiating from this leaf rosette on long stems are 'pussy paws'—fuzzy, round clusters of many of the crepe-papery, rose to cream flowers.

Typical location: rocky flats and ridges, e.g., 2nd Burroughs Mt. (7300').

Distribution: 5000–14,000'—Cascades and coastal mountains from southern British Columbia to northern California; Sierra Nevada; Great Basin; Rockies.

Names: *Calyptridium* means 'cap' in reference to the uniting of the petals into a cap-like structure when the flower is in fruit. *Umbellatum* means 'forming an umbel.'

■ rose (white)
● 4 separate petals in spherical cluster
✿ July–August

PINK/RED• 5 PETALS   *Castilleja rupicola*

Cliff Paintbrush

Typical location: rocky ridges and flats, e.g., rocky slope along lower part of trail to 1st Burroughs Mt. (6900').

Distribution: 6800–9000'— Cascades from southern British Columbia to Oregon.

Names: *Castilleja* (see p. 91). *Rupicola* (see p. 104).

Both cliff paintbrush in the alpine fellfields and magenta paintbrush (p. 131) in the subalpine meadows dazzle and amaze with their intense, vibrant colors. Cliff paintbrush is a short plant (to 8"), but you can see its brilliant color igniting alpine ridges and flats for what seems like miles. • As with all paintbrushes, the color comes from the bracts. **Unlike most paintbrush flowers, those of cliff paintbrush are not hidden**—the green 'snout' holding the reproductive parts sticks out ½–1" beyond the bracts (see lower photo). • The leaves are 5-lobed and, as with most alpine plants, white-hairy.

- red
- 5 petals united in a 2-lipped tube
- July–August

Pedicularis ornithorhyncha

5 PETALS • PINK/RED

Bird's-beak Lousewort

Bird's-beak lousewort is another of the peculiar *Pedicularis* species that inhabit the meadows, slopes, and ridges of Rainier. As with the others of its kind (pp. 119, 125, 150, 167), the 2 petals of the upper lip unite to form a 'beak,' but in bird's-beak lousewort the beak does not curve up or twist to the side but curves straight down, mimicking a duck's head and bill. The 3 petals of the lower lip are usually lighter pink and form a flap that bends down, appearing a bit like the front of the duck's body. • The 3–12" stems are smooth up to the inflorescence, beyond which they are covered with short, white hairs. The 1–5" basal leaves are deeply lobed and toothed (fern-like); there are a few much smaller stem leaves. Most of the 'ducks' flock together in a dense cluster at the top of the stem; a few others are attached to the stem a little lower down.

Typical location: meadows and rocky slopes, e.g., along trail up 1st Burroughs Mt. (7000'). Also found in upper subalpine zone.

Distribution: 6000–8000'—Cascades and coastal mountains from British Columbia to Washington.

Names: *Pedicularis* (see p. 119). *Ornithorhyncha* means 'shaped like a bird's beak.'

- red-purple (pink)
- 5 petals united in a 2-lipped tube
- ✿ July–August

SNAPDRAGON FAMILY

PINK/RED • 5 PETALS   *Silene acaulis*

Moss Campion

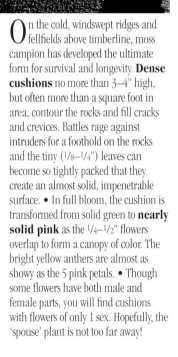

Typical location: rocky flats and rock crevices, e.g., along trail up 1st Burroughs Mt. (7000').

Distribution: 5000–10,000'— Cascades and coastal mountains from Alaska to Oregon; Rockies; across Canada and northern U.S.

Names: *Silene* is one of those rather obscure genus names, probably deriving from Silenus, foster-father of Bacchus. *Acaulis* means 'stemless,' as these miniature plants almost are.

■ pink
● 5 petals united at base
✿ July–August

On the cold, windswept ridges and fellfields above timberline, moss campion has developed the ultimate form for survival and longevity. **Dense cushions** no more than 3–4" high, but often more than a square foot in area, contour the rocks and fill cracks and crevices. Battles rage against intruders for a foothold on the rocks and the tiny ($1/8$–$1/4$") leaves can become so tightly packed that they create an almost solid, impenetrable surface. • In full bloom, the cushion is transformed from solid green to **nearly solid pink** as the $1/4$–$1/2$" flowers overlap to form a canopy of color. The bright yellow anthers are almost as showy as the 5 pink petals. • Though some flowers have both male and female parts, you will find cushions with flowers of only 1 sex. Hopefully, the 'spouse' plant is not too far away!

Phlox diffusa

Spreading Phlox

In any rocky place in Rainier, from the upper reaches of the forest zone to the highest ridges and fellfields above timberline, you will be likely to find spreading phlox. Its ¹/₂–³/₄" **star-shaped flowers paint the rocks with pastels from pink to lavender to white**. • The branches spread horizontally, creating loose mats that rarely exceed a few inches tall. Flowers may be scattered on the mat or growing so profusely that the leaves are completely hidden beneath them. The short (¹/₂") **leaves are needle-like** and grow thickly on the branches in fused pairs. • One of the earliest and longest bloomers in the rocks (regardless of elevation), phlox is a spectacular herald of the arrival of the blooming season and a constant and delightful companion throughout summer.

Typical location: rocky ridges and outcrops, talus slopes, e.g., along trail up 1st Burroughs Mt. (7000'). Also found in upper forest and subalpine zones.

Distribution: 3500–12,000'— Cascades and coastal mountains from southern British Columbia to northern California; eastern Washington; Sierra Nevada; northern Rockies.

Names: *Phlox* means 'flame' in reference to the often bright flowers. *Diffusa* means 'spreading' in reference to the plant's mat growth form.

■ pink (lavender or white)
● 5 petals united at base into a tube
❀ June–August

BLUE/PURPLE • 5 PETALS   *Penstemon davidsonii*

Davidson's Penstemon

Typical location: rocky slopes and flats, e.g., rocky slope along trail up 2nd Burroughs Mt. (7300'). Also found in upper subalpine zone.

Distribution: 5500–12,000'— Cascades and coastal mountains from southern British Columbia to northern California; Sierra Nevada.

Names: *Penstemon* (see p.104). George Davidson was a collector of western plants.

■ blue-purple (lavender)
● 5 petals united in a
   2-lipped tube
✿ July–August

Davidson's penstemon is one of the great joys of the alpine flora. A mat of Davidson's penstemon in full bloom is glorious, especially in the rather austere, rocky environment it frequents. It looks like a band of hundreds of lavender trumpets blaring out of the ground. • The tubular flowers are unusually large (1–1½") for an alpine plant and appear even larger because the stems are only a few inches high and the leathery leaves are only ½" long and wide. The plant **often forms extensive mats (several feet across) dense with flowers** that usually grow erect on their stems. • The flowers can vary from lavender blue to deep purple with throats and anthers that are white-hairy or wooly; the entire inflorescence is glandular.

Lupinus lepidus var. *lobbii*

5 PETALS • BLUE/PURPLE

Alpine Lupine

It's truly a stunning sight to see an otherwise bare, rocky slope above timberline covered with a **mini-forest of bright blue** alpine lupine. Though the plant is dwarfed (1–4" tall), almost all of its height is thick with the ½" blue flowers. • Alpine lupine usually forms extensive mats, its tiny ¼–½", basal leaves almost completely covering the ground for several square yards.

• The silky-hairy **leaves are palmately compound** with 5–9 narrow leaflets. The upper erect petal (the banner) is the same deep blue as the other petals but has a bright white 'eye' in its center. Standing near a mat of alpine lupine can make you feel like you are being watched by hundreds of inquisitive lupine eyes.

Typical location: rocky ridges and flats, scree slopes, e.g., along trail to 1st Burroughs Mt. (7000'), masses of plants on Wonderland Trail near Panhandle Gap (6700'). Also found in upper subalpine zone.

Distribution: 6000–11,000'— Cascades and coastal mountains from British Columbia to northern California; Sierra Nevada.

Names: *Lupinus* (see p.133). *Lepidus* means 'elegant.' Also known as dwarf lupine and *L. lyallii*.

■ blue
● 5 irregular petals (banner, wings, keel)
✿ July–August

PEA FAMILY

BLUE/PURPLE• 5 PETALS   *Polemonium elegans*

Elegant Jacob's Ladder

Typical location: rocky slopes and around rocks, e.g., in rocks along trail up 1st Burroughs Mt. (7000').

Distribution: above 6000'— Cascades and coastal mountains from British Columbia to northern California; Rockies.

Names: *Polemonium* (see p.137). *Elegans* means 'elegant.' Also known as sky pilot.

■ blue
● 5 petals united in a bowl
✿ July–August

If you love the beautiful blue flowers of showy Jacob's ladder (*P. pulcherrimum*, p.137), found around trees on the edges of subalpine meadows, you will be delighted to know that even when you are on rocky slopes above the tree limit, the blossoms of Jacob's ladder may still be with you. • Elegant Jacob's ladder has very similar flowers to those of showy Jacob's ladder— **rich blue or blue-purple with bright yellow or orange 'bull's-eye' centers**. *P. elegans* is a more compact plant than *P. pulcherrimum* with clusters of flowers at the ends of stems that rarely exceed 6". •The leaves consist of many pairs of small 'ladder-rung' leaflets, which are tiny (1/4"), numerous (13–27 pairs), and tightly crowded together to create **leaves that resemble braided mouse tails**.

Aster alpigenus

Alpine Aster

Alpine aster almost seems out of place in the rocky tundra above the tree limit; its gorgeous blue (to purple or lavender) flowerheads are enormous compared to most alpine flowers. While 1/2" or smaller is typical for alpine flowers, these stunning asters may be **up to 1 1/2" across**! • The narrow leaves are mostly basal and are a rich green that tends to turn purplish with age. The 2–16" stems are reddish and white-hairy. The **15–40 blue-purple rays** surround a bright yellow-orange 'button' of many disk flowers. • The phyllaries under the flowerhead are long and slender and form several overlapping rows.

Typical location: rocky slopes and flats, e.g., along trail up 1st Burroughs Mt. (7000'). Also found in subalpine zone.

Distribution: 5000–10,000'— Cascades and coastal mountains from Washington to northern California; Sierra Nevada; Rockies.

Names: *Aster* means 'star.' *Alpigenus* means 'of the alpine.'

■ blue-purple
● many ray and disk flowers
✿ July–August

COMPOSITE FAMILY

Glossary

alien: not native; introduced into an area

anther: the pollen-producing tip of the male part of a flower

axil: where the leaf stalk joins the plant stem

banner: the upper petal of a pea flower, e.g., subalpine lupine, p. 133

basal leaves: the leaves located at the stem base, e.g., rusty saxifrage, p. 101

bract: a leaf-like structure performing a different function from that of a leaf, e.g., the non-green leaf-like structures on the upper stems of paintbrush, pp. 91, 131, 176, or the showy white petal-like structures of Canadian dogwood, p. 41

bulbil: a small, bulb-like reproductive structure often located in a leaf axil, which falls to the ground and sprouts

calyx: a collective term for the sepals

carpel: a single pistil or modified leaf bearing undeveloped seeds

circumboreal: distributed around the globe in high latitudes

clasping: holding or surrounding tightly, e.g., leaves clasping the stem

corolla: collective term for the petals

cushion plant: a plant of the alpine zone with densely packed, ground-hugging leaves, e.g., moss campion, p. 178

disk flowers: in the composite family, the small, tubular flowers comprising the 'button' in the center of the flowerhead; some composites have only disk flowers, e.g., alpine pussytoes, p. 169

dioecious: flowers that are unisexual with staminate and pistillate flowers borne on separate plants, e.g., goat's beard, p. 82

fellfield: a type of tundra that is 35–50% bare rock, with existing vegetation consisting of cushion plants, mosses, and lichens

filament: the stalk of the male part of the flower that bears the anther at its tip

follicle: a dry, single-carled fruit that splits to release the seeds

forest line: the elevation where thick, contiguous forest ends

glandular: bearing glands; sticky

hybridization: cross-breeding of different species

inferior ovary: an ovary situated below the petals, e.g., fireweed, p. 88

inflorescence: an entire cluster of flowers and associated structures

involucre: group of bracts under a flower, cluster of flowers, or fruit

mat plant: a plant with loosely packed, ground-hugging leaves, e.g., arctic sandwort, p. 164

palmately compound leaves: having leaflets all arising from the same point (like the fingers of the hand), e.g., subalpine lupine, p. 133

panicle: a branched inflorescence, e.g., brook saxifrage, p. 71

parasitic: obtaining food and nutrients from living organisms

pedicel: a flower stalk

perianth: a collective term for the petals and sepals together

petiole: a leaf stalk

phyllary: one of the narrow, usually green, bracts forming the cup under the flowerhead of a composite, e.g., alpine golden daisy, p. 172

pinnately compound leaves: having leaflets on both sides of the common axis, like ladderrungs, e.g., showy Jacob's ladder, p. 137

pistil: the female part of the flower, including the ovary, style, and stigma

pistillate flowers: flowers with fertile pistils but sterile or missing stamens

raceme: an unbranched inflorescence with stalked flowers along an elongated axis, e.g., monkshood, p. 78

ray flowers: the wide-flaring flowers (rays) of members of the composite family, e.g., broadleaf arnica, p. 127

reflexed: abruptly bent or curved back or down

rhizome: an underground, horizontal stem

rosette: a radiating cluster of leaves usually at or near ground level, e.g., pussypaws, p. 175

saprophytic: obtaining food and nutrients from dead or decaying matter

scree: a slope or field of small rocks

sepals: the typically green parts beneath the petals; the protective layer around the bud

stamen: the male structure, consisting of the filament and the anther

staminate flowers: having fertile stamens but sterile or missing pistils

staminode: a sterile stamen

stigma: the tip of the female part that is receptive to pollen

superior ovary: an ovary situated above the petals

style: the thin stalk connecting the ovary and the stigma of the female structure

sub-shrub: a plant with woody lower stems and non-woody upper stems and twigs that die back seasonally, e.g., partridge foot, p. 165

talus: a slope or field of large rocks or boulders

tepal: sepals and petals that are alike in appearance, e.g., queen's cup, p. 36

tree limit: the elevation above which no trees (even dwarfed ones) grow

tundra: treeless plains or flats above or north of the tree limit

umbel: an inflorescence in which the flower stalks arise from a common point (umbrella-like), e.g., cow parsnip, p. 143

unisexual: having flowers where either the stamens or pistils, but not both, are fertile, e.g., goat's beard, p. 82

whorled: arranged in rings of 3 or more, e.g., tiger lily, p. 86

Scientific Names Index

Common Names Index

A

Agoseris
    orange, 87
    short-beaked, 173
Alumroot, small-flowered, 100
Anemone, western. *See* pasqueflower
Arnica
    boadleaf, 127
    mountain. *See* broadleaf arnica
Aster
    alpine, 183
    Cascade, 138

B

Balm, western. See pennyroyal
Beadlily. See queen's cup
Beadruby. *See* false lily-of-the-valley
Bearberry. *See* kinnikinnick
Beard-tongue, woodland. *See*
    woodland penstemon
Beargrass, 118
Betony, wood. *See* bracted lousewort
Bistort, 142
Bluebell, tall, 77
Bluebells of Scotland. *See* common
    harebell
Blueberry
    delicious. *See* Cascade huckleberry
    oval-leaf, 61
Bramble, dwarf. *See* creeping
    raspberry
Bride's bonnet. See queen's cup
Bugbane, false, 72
Bunchberry. See Canadian dogwood
Butterbur. *See* sweet coltsfoot
Butterwort, 76

C

Campion, moss, 178
Candystick, 43

Cinquefoil
    fan-leaf, 126
    Rainier. *See* fan-leaf cinquefoil
    shrubby, 171
Coltsfoot
    sweet, 145
    tall, 145
Columbine, crimsone, 94
Coralroot
    Merten's. *See* western coralroot
    western, 57
Corydalis, western, 89

D

Daisy
    alpine golden, 172
    mountain, 123
    subalpine. *See* mountain daisy
Dandelion, orange mounain. *See*
    orange agoseris
Devil's club, 51
Dogwood, Canadian, 41

E

Elephantsheads, 150
Elmera, 163
Everlasting, pearly, 85

F

Fairy slipper, 58
Fairybell, Hooker's, 38
False Solomon's seal
    plumose , 66
    star-flowered, 66
Fireweed, 88
Foamflower, 48
Foxglove, 93
Fringecup, 69

About the Author

Laird has led wildflower field classes in the mountains of the American West for over 20 years. With *Wildflowers of Mt. Rainier* now joining his previous two highly successful wildflower field guides—*Wildflowers of the Tahoe Sierra* and *Wildflowers of the Sierra Nevada and the Central Valley*—he has brought some of his favorite flowers and most cherished places to word and image.

In his other life, Laird is professor of psychology, literature, and ecology at Sierra Nevada College—a small piece of academic heaven nestled in the mountains of Lake Tahoe.